COUNTRY LIVING

Your House,
Your Home

COUNTRY LIVING

Your House, Your Home

Randy Florke's
Decorating Essentials

Randy Florke with
Nancy J. Becker

Hearst Books
A Division of Sterling Publishing Co., Inc.
New York

Design by Margaret Rubiano

Library of Congress Cataloging-in-Publication Data
Available upon request.

10   9   8   7   6   5   4   3   2   1

First Paperback Edition 2006
Published by Hearst Books
A Division of Sterling Publishing Co., Inc.
387 Park Avenue South, New York, NY 10016

Country Living and Hearst Books are trademarks of Hearst Communications, Inc.

www.countryliving.com

For information about custom editions, special sales, premium and corporate purchases, please contact Sterling Special Sales Department at 800-805-5489 or specialsales@sterlingpub.com.

Distributed in Canada by Sterling Publishing
c/o Canadian Manda Group, 165 Dufferin Street
Toronto, Ontario, Canada M6K 3H6

Distributed in Australia by Capricorn Link (Australia) Pty. Ltd.
P.O. Box 704, Windsor, NSW 2756 Australia

Manufactured in China

Sterling ISBN 13: 978-1-58816-608-1
            ISBN 10: 1-58816-608-2

To Sean, Jesus, Daley, and Essie:
Without you a house is not a home.

Contents

Foreword

I first learned about Randy Florke about five years ago through photos of his home in the Catskill Mountains of New York. The house had a personality. It was filled with a casual exuberance: worn furniture, soft colors, and easy, comfortable upholstery combined with a simple sense of style. There was a great deal of integrity too, allowing the bare bones of the farmhouse to come alive while remaining true to the farmhouse spirit. I had two thoughts: first, that this house should be in the pages of *Country Living* magazine, and second, who was Randy Florke and how was he able to transform this simple, neglected farmhouse into a stylish yet accessible haven? Our first face-to-face meeting was over lunch. Tall, blond, handsome, and originally from Iowa, I soon discovered that Randy was the real deal. He spoke of his love of simple furniture that has stories to tell, of his pride in the farmhouse and its rough-hewn patina, and of the beauty and power of working with what you have to create your own sense of style. His belief in creating homes that are comfortable and accessible fits perfectly with

Country Living magazine. Since that meeting we have continued to work together. I've never seen anybody renovate a house (with quality and integrity) as fast as Randy. He has a vision for each home that he renovates on behalf of his clients and for each house that he transforms for himself and his family. His method is swift, decisive, and always on course. In this book, Randy discusses and simplifies decorating, room by room. He takes you through his three principles of design and then shows how to apply them to your own home and space. And best of all, he'll take you through the wonderful personal journey he has traveled in creating homes that are filled with comfort, and style. I know you'll enjoy it, be informed and inspired, as I was when I first met Randy—and still am today.

— Nancy Mernit Soriano
Editor-in-Chief, *Country Living*

Introduction

Home is a place you grow up wanting to leave, and grow old wanting to go back to.
—John Ed Pearce,
Louisville Courier Journal Magazine

◀ I passed this Iowa farmhouse every day on my way to school. Who knew I'd one day own it?

For as long as I can remember,

I sat on the right side of the school bus in the morning, and the other side on the way home. The reason for my obsession with seating arrangements was a worn gray clapboard farmhouse and a scattered collection of outbuildings, including guesthouse and barn, all set back from the road. I studied the farmhouse's shingled roof and enclosed porch and marveled at the tall farmer's windmill rising from a cluster of fruit trees. Smoke curled from one of two brick chimneys, and what appeared to be lace hung from the second tier of a neat row of windows. I wanted to live in that house. I was ten years old.

Years later, nearing thirty and having lived in Spain, Iowa called me home again. My thoughts went immediately to the gray clapboard farmhouse set back from the road. Some folks dream of penthouses, island retreats, lodges near fashionable resorts, but those years on a school bus dipping up and down country roads informed me: I wanted a farm—that gray clapboard house in particular—but was it for sale, and if so, could I afford it?

You haven't dealt in real estate until you've bargained with an Iowan farmer over a

A Hidden Treasure

Vintage athletic equipment, such as the hockey skates slung on the headboard in my son's room, is commonly found at garage sales and flea markets. Collections begin with that first serendipitous find. Look for old catcher's masks, bowling pins, colorful pool balls, or vintage wooden bats.

▶ This iron bedstead, exhumed from the grounds of the Iowa farmhouse, probably had been buried for forty years.

homestead tangled with holdover tenants and lifetime rights. Because he didn't live there, and because he didn't think he could reach an advantageous agreement, his initial response to my query of what he intended to do with the place was "Burn it down." My look of panic, plus my blurting out for him to name his price, must have touched him somewhere in his hardscrabble Iowan soul. "Sixteen thousand

▲ The Iowa farmhouse called for hardy furnishings, such as this old pine cabinet and painted farmer's table, as the house would be left unattended for long periods. Note the colorful tower of cigar boxes.

dollars," said he; "Yes," said I. I had purchased my first American dream.

During tough, personal crises, some people turn to therapy, others to drink. I had ended an important relationship, returned to New York from Spain, and purchased a broken-down farmhouse in Iowa, the better days for which seemed behind it. I threw myself into a frenzy of renovation and restoration and found that, lo and behold, more than just a homestead was restored. Working with your hands can mend a heart. It doesn't happen overnight, but neither does a renovation.

I filled the rooms with simple, hand-hewn, prairie furniture: solid pine farmer's tables and oak dressers, chipped mirrors and hutches made from barnyard scrap. Nothing had a pedigree, but each was practical and procured locally from thrift stores and church bazaars and family members' basements and attics. Ever alert to the detritus of others, I made good use of found objects. In the past, Midwestern farmers were known to bury their refuse in some outlying corner of the homestead; this was, after all, before municipal trash removal. Metal objects and pottery can survive years entombed underground. And there's nothing like the patina bestowed by good farm soil. A prize find included a rustic iron bedstead, now taking pride of place in my son's room.

The philosophy behind my *mise-en-scène* is one of comfort and accessibility: I want a room to pull me in, welcome me with the warmth of a patchwork quilt or braided rug and the familiarity of lost yet longed-for objects. Being surrounded by the practical artifacts of the past—enameled colanders, milkware pitchers,

a mismatched set of Bakelite-handled utensils—instills in me the pride of thrift and creates connections to pasts, sometimes only fictional. I wonder who held these things before me? What preoccupation accounted for the chip in a favorite blue bowl? It's fun to guess about the provenance of an object and perhaps make up a story or two.

Having been raised in Iowa, the purchase of what became known as Cottonwood Creek Farm was a return of sorts to the people who'd raised me. I needed a place for my own growing family when Iowa reunions called the multi-generational clan to roost. But New York City was my permanent home, and visits to Iowa would be sporadic. The farm would have to be tough, low-maintenance, able to bear the smudges of little fingers and long cold winter months on its own. Not only did I find a sturdy little house with a pioneering spirit, I filled it with the stuff of fruit cellars and barn lofts, which, refreshed with a fast coat of paint, seemed grateful to take up prime positions indoors. I discovered that I liked things Iowan. In the past I'd been known to downplay my midwestern roots. But now the ordinary household objects of a farmer's wife—flour sifters, rolling pins, tin breadboxes—seemed important: rugged, practical, worthy of a new respect. Suddenly the solidity of the farmhouse, its stalwart underpinnings and good bones, appealed to me. I was home. I was really home.

In this volume, I will explore what I call the three muses of design: comfort, economy, and color. And what do my muses look like? Well, comfort wears fresh plaid gingham, lives in embroidered cotton bedclothes, and sports oft-washed linen and line-dried quilts. Comfort is an overstuffed sofa dressed casually in thick, pet-friendly fabric. Economy might mean previously owned or found objects from flea markets, thrift stores, or a grandmother's attic. Economy is a vignette of mismatched ladder-back chairs, painted off-white, grouped around a rustic farm table. Economy employs objects with integrity: things that worked then and still work now. And color? Color is the faded blue of country crockery; it is the ivories, whites, and yellows of damask tablecloths and hand-stitched pillowcases. Color can be the red of apples in a green ceramic bowl and the muted grays of original bead board and worn garden sculpture.

Many people are surprised at the items I choose on thrift-store or flea-market outings. "What are you going to do with that old thing?" someone invariably asks, as I plunk down money for a paint-chipped table. Those same folks seem delighted with the pleasant interiors of mismatched furniture, gently used fabrics, and sun-washed colors that somehow manage to emerge from the junk. I'd like to help people develop their innate sense of seeing. By seeing I mean the ability to cut through the visual clutter and homogeneity of the marketplace and select and gather objects of integrity and style. Developing a visual sense is not about money and it's not about hopping on the next bandwagon. It is about what you like . . . making lists of colors, textures, and objects you want to collect, then learning how to search and buy.

Join me as I explore ways to decorate with style and thrift, transforming the ordinary room into a place of extraordinary personal charm. Whether you're decorating an entire house or simply freshening a tired room, each chapter offers real-life examples, room by room, of my adventures with old homes and found objects. See if you agree with my ideas for each room and develop your own. Learn how to apply my tenets of design to the specific challenges in your home, and look for the "Quick Fix" sections which offer cheap, fast solutions. Develop the confidence to employ a thrifty rather than costly solution, to choose the unique rather than the tried and true. Create rooms of originality and comfort,

The Three Muses of Design

- ■ Comfort

- ■ Economy

- ■ Color

◀ Perhaps it was also the memory of the farmer's windmill that drew me back to Iowa.

rooms you're just dying to come home to, rooms that are a welcoming refuge from the busy world.

Remember that most of the ideas in this book work in any style of house, whether ranch, colonial, contemporary, or turn of the century. Don't be afraid to try something just because you don't happen to own a late-nineteenth-century farmhouse.

Meet the Houses

Since the houses that have come and gone in my life are sort of like characters from a novel—and will make their appearance from time to time in these pages—I'd like to introduce each one. You've already met the sturdy and reliable Cottonwood Creek Farm, my midwestern homestead. Hunkered down on ten acres of nontillable soil in Cherokee County, Iowa, the Cottonwood Creek house is a plain-faced, clapboard dwelling that was erected in 1890.

▼ Cottonwood Creek Farm . . . the house that started it all.

But don't let the simple, bare-boned countenance of this house fool you: it's withstood windstorms and cold fronts as well as drenchings and droughts, all with nary a whimper. A stalwart companion, it will be here long after me.

Some houses have grand provenances or pedigrees: important architects, famous owners, historic guests. Others are of more humble origins, and such is the case of Wilken Farm in Callicoon, New York. Built to house a farmer and his brood in 1910, this working farm once sat on hundreds of acres before being whittled down to a mere twenty-two. A county road was built, cleaving the land in two and running close

▼ The Mohn Road house in Cochecton, New York, features a wonderful wraparound porch and a visit from Casper, our neighbor's friendly goat.

▼ Wilken Farm did time as a boarding house but has been restored to its former beauty.

enough to the building to make a boarding house feasible in the grim economic climate of the 1930s. But the clapboard façade, working shutters, two porches, and sunroom survived, and the original five-bedroom farmhouse emerged gloriously in the restoration.

If there is a genteel and well-bred aunt among this cast of characters it would be the Mohn Road house in Cochecton, New York. The air of the Victorians wafts about this dwelling: there are touches of primness in the scalloped shingles, sharp window peaks, and trim, wraparound porch. One looks out on gently undulating hills of green from a perch on the huge wooden rocker. Although country-bred, there is a touch of the formal in its three-storied stateliness.

The witty bachelor enters this story in the guise of my Washington, D.C., townhouse, erected in 1890. Even the name of the neighborhood in which it's found sounds masculine: Adams Morgan, located less than a mile from the White House. If there's a bit of the rogue in the D.C. townhouse, it is the approachable, attractive rogue; the desirable, waiting-to-be-married-off Jane Austen hero sort of rogue. With its gray façade, arched brickwork, and Seaton Street address, there is something of the London row house about it,

▶ Gray was an unusual choice for a façade, but I think it works for the Washington, D.C., townhouse.

not exactly formal but able to be dressed up and opened to any or all of society.

If "flow"—that ineffable quality that draws occupants and guests alike comfortably from room to room—is important in a house, the Jeffersonville, New York, house has it in spades. This is the welcoming and garrulous uncle of the group: comfortable in its own skin, well designed, sun-drenched. Remotely located when it was built in 1910, the house sat calmly as the center of town crept closer. Now it has adapted to society and treats all who enter to an understated elegance with such features as multiple sets of French doors, both open and glassed-in porches, and ornate, early-twentieth-century light fixtures.

Our next character is something of a hybrid: part 1820 parish house with an equal dose of the utterly modern thrown in. You see, my brand-new modular construction in Youngsville, New York, is a member of the new generation. I took inspiration from an early-twentieth-century house that clung to the edge of a cemetery, then drew up plans so that the bones of the house could be constructed in a factory. With the addition of period details, such as wainscoting, wide plank floors, bead-board ceilings, radiators and muse-inspired objects, fabrics and colors, . . . voilá: brand-new

▶ Nearly everything had to be re-created inside the Harlem row house, but the exterior clapboard siding and original wooden stoop were saved.

construction and a finished home that looks anything but new.

Location scouts must have been as thrilled as I to discover Sylvan Terrace in New York City's Harlem, as it represents nearly perfect examples of late-nineteenth-century wood row houses, all identical and lined up on a dead-ended, cobblestoned street. Of the fifteen or so houses, very little has been altered: the ubiquitous wood stoops and railings; tall, raised-panel double-front doors; and working, wood-slatted shutters all remain intact. The Morris-Jumel Mansion, a Tuscan-columned, one-time headquarters for none other than George Washington, stands regally to the east, providing a wonderful backdrop for films

purporting to take place as early as 1765. The Harlem townhouse is an urban retreat, a tad reclusive; it's bundled in shoulder-to-shoulder with its like-minded neighbors on a fairy-tale street, free of traffic and storefronts—an unusual enclave in an otherwise anonymous city.

Now that they have been properly introduced, let's proceed with the plot. Each home was a labor of love, unique in the challenges and adventures presented to this intrepid refurbisher. I'll go room by room. And please forgive the odd flight of fancy into childhood memories and fondly recalled dreams in these pages. There are muses about after all.

—Randy Florke

(Please note, before you begin any project, read the Appendix for a discussion of general safety precautions.)

▼ The most welcoming of all my houses: the Jeffersonville house. Local produce, in this case pumpkins, adds to the cheer.

▼ Many are surprised to learn that my parish-inspired house is of totally new construction.

Gathering Places—
Kitchens

*No matter where I serve my guests, it
seems they like my kitchen best.*
—Cross-Stitch Proverb

◀ An impromptu island (an industrial table) is
anchored by a patch of sisal while the wonderful
enameled Magic Chef stove takes center stage.

Given the choice of luxurious

seating in a spacious living room or bundling in groups in a tight little kitchen, most guests will opt for the latter. What is the draw, the allure of a kitchen? Is it the bright accessibility? Is it the kitchen's position, often, as the hub and heart of the residence, a place where much of the day's activity begins? Could it simply be the kitchen's standing as a place of sustenance and comfort? Kitchens are where we stir our oatmeal and warm our cocoa; we nourish our children there

and feed our pets there. As impressed as I am by the sleek modernity of the newfangled stainless-steel refrigerators and slick granite countertops, a kitchen, to me, should be a warm and welcoming cocoon of ease and familiarity. I don't want chilly floors, sharp edges, and stark countertops; I want to be soothed, warmed, and brought gently into the day.

Before I began the renovation of my first kitchen—in an Iowan farmhouse built in 1890—I thought about the kitchens in my past. For more than forty years, the same enamel-topped table held a prime place in my grandmother's kitchen. It could be extended to accommodate the entire family, and with its solid wooden base and perfect height, I thought it most useful. My grandmother, too,

A Hidden Treasure

Miniatures charm—whether birdhouses, or small architectural models, such as this wooden house. I placed it on the lower tier of the kitchen island for a glimpse of the unexpected (see previous page).

▶ By foregoing curtains for the windows and door, I've ushered in natural light to keep the Iowa kitchen bright.

Home Comforts for a Kitchen

- **Light:** Try a single-panel French or Dutch door in the kitchen to let in all available light.

- **Ample workspace:** Add a butcher block or island of industrial shelves to expand usable space.

- **Storage:** Rustic corner cabinets, hutches, or pie safes look great in country kitchens.

- **Seating:** Mismatched ladder-back chairs all painted white are an economical and decorative solution.

- **Cheer:** Employ old-time advertising signage for a sense of whimsy.

saw the table as sound and serviceable, so as those around her updated their kitchens with brand-new maple sets, she saw no need to replace it. My grandmother's resistance to change, simply for the sake of change itself, impressed me, as did her loyalty to the unpretentious and useful objects of the 1920s, '30s, and '40s. My grandmother was accused of being frugal and stuck in the past, but I adopted her sense of economy and comfort as two important tenets of my approach to design.

A Thoughtful Renovation
Above and Below—Floors and Ceilings

Nearly everyone wants to renovate his or her kitchen at some point. This shouldn't mean that everything original be done away with. For obvious reasons of economy, I try to work with what the room already has and simply do a bit of editing. While older kitchens may have many troublesome features that call for modernization, there will invariably be things that can be saved. The fine art of editing requires an eye for things that work, things that pull their weight. Wood floors, enormous ceramic basins, glass-doored cabinetry might all be wonderfully incorporated into an older kitchen's refreshening. I nearly always pull up linoleum or abused old flooring

◀ A glass-paneled French door lets in the light to my Washington, D.C., townhouse kitchen. Note also the tin bread box placed high atop the cabinet to draw the eye up, thus underscoring the sense of vertical space.

and often find pine or oak floorboards underneath. Since the Iowa farmhouse is used only as a vacation retreat, I sanded then oiled the original pine floor. Though not an ideal solution for high-traffic areas because of the difficult upkeep, this works well in a vacation home.

Before removing linoleum, investigate the source of adhesion. At Wilken Farm in Sullivan County, New York, I foolishly scraped the linoleum on hands and knees, only to discover that it had been glued to plywood. Of course the plywood had to come up, so inadvertently I had added a labor-intense yet unnecessary step. Underneath the plywood were beautiful knotty pine floors wonderfully preserved. So don't be immediately turned off by a room with linoleum; it may have played the role of protector to the exquisite wood beneath. On the other hand, you could choose to keep it intact. Authentic

◀ The pinewood floors in the kitchen in the Iowa farmhouse were sanded and oiled, and the Sheetrock ceiling was then painted white.

❧ A Hidden Treasure

A small braided rug adds a dash of country. This particular rug is a treasured memento of my grandmother's handicraft, but you might easily snag one at a flea market or auction.

linoleum, in good shape and in an interesting color, could set the stage for a 1950s retro look, with a bulbous refrigerator and an enamel and chrome-trimmed stove. Look for the larger square examples that have a marbled look. What fun you could have with the color scheme of that decade, such as turquoise, pale green, or even pink and black.

In contrast, the more formal and more heavily trafficked maple floors of the Mohn Road house were sanded, stained, and polyurethaned. I tend toward satin-finish rather than high-gloss when it comes to wood floors. However my rule of thumb is to apply two coats of high-gloss with a final coat of satin finish. The high gloss dries harder and provides a smooth surface on which to lay the flatter finish. I like the simplicity and warmth of wood floors,

particularly in the kitchen. And with the large supply of wood-treatment products on the market today, there's no reason to fear wood floors there. The old admonition "Water on wood, no good" can be quickly forgotten.

Most dropped ceilings have to go. Doing so brings height and light to the kitchen. What you do after the dropped ceiling is removed will depend on what you find. A punched-tin ceiling, in good shape, would be a gift, although I've yet to discover one. Replications of tin in molded man-made materials that are applied in sheets are available and are actually difficult to tell apart from originals. For most of my ceilings, I install Sheetrock and then paint. If the original lath/plaster ceiling is fit for paint, then I by all means retain it.

Store It—Cabinetry

In a kitchen renovation, a key decision is whether to use the cabinets you've got or to replace them. I've done both and been satisfied with the results. At the Wilken house I was met with the typical flat cabinets of the 1950s; sound as far as shape yet dull in terms of style. I removed the undistinguished hardware and, in order to add interest, applied thin wooden frames and wainscot paneling to the face of the cabinets. The pieces were glued on and tacked in place

with tiny brads. If you choose this approach, the frames and wainscot paneling can be as simple or as fancy as you like. Before painting the entire unit, I added simple wooden knobs; if you prefer the country-hutch feeling of glass doors, you can remove the center panels from your old cabinets and have glass installed. Add a frame of molding around the glass, and the ordinary is transformed to the extraordinary. However, if what you've got simply has to go, you can purchase inexpensive, plain-Jane cabinets at most large home-furnishings retailers and then doctor them with wainscoting or molding. I took that road in the Harlem townhouse kitchen, and the cabinets are streamlined and clean-looking.

Another alternative for larger country kitchens is to replace built-in cabinets with freestanding hutches and corner cupboards. Look for good, strong pieces with ample shelf space at flea markets or antique stores. Glass-doored cabinets look great in the kitchen; or, remove the doors entirely from an antique cupboard for easy access to dishes and such. (Remember to retain some space in which the interior contents may be hidden. We all have kitchen gadgets and housewares that are better left offstage. You could cover some glass doors with lace, vintage fabric,

▼ Wooden frames and knobs added to a plain cabinet made for a finished-looking island (foreground); white paint helped. The pantry was made from an old bookshelf with a simple screen door attached. My French bulldog, Ronco, checks it all out.

or old wallpaper.) Islands or butcher blocks can also add much-needed workspace in a busy kitchen. Check out the nearest restaurant supply store for a used butcher block, or build your own island like I did. For the Mohn Road house kitchen, I attached a set of industrial wheels to the bottom of a primitive cabinet, refaced the backside, placed a large slab of wood on the top, and voilà; instant island. And movable, too. (Remember to include engagable brakes on at least two of the wheels so that the island can be safely locked in place.)

Many people put up with having insufficient workspace in the kitchen, but it's one of my minimum daily requirements. In the Harlem kitchen, I wanted cement countertops for a streamlined, clean look, so I had forms built and the cement poured on site. A skilled mason can provide a smooth surface. Other less costly options are simple wood-plank countertops that can be purchased prefabricated at many home-renovation outlets.

A Hidden Treasure

The surprise that an indoor birdhouse engenders is part of the fun of decorating. I love the weather-beaten ones that have done serious time out of doors.

▼ A glass-doored hutch added to the kitchen in Iowa was freshened with a coat of paint.

Color—
A Subtle Muse

Since many of the objects that I collect are rich in color, to display them well I often use bright whites, off-whites, or pale yellows on kitchen walls. Pale hues seem an ideal backdrop for the sturdy country furniture I cast in the integral roles of comfort and utility. The furniture itself can be dark wood, which contrasts nicely against white walls, or it can wear a coat of white paint to harmonize with the pale background. White is a clean, soothing color and instantly accepts not only variations of itself but also any member of the larger palette. Much as an artist might, I begin with a canvas of white, then choose

▼ The white walls and brown wood of the Iowa house kitchen and dining rooms are a nice contrast; note how the painted chairs stand out against the dark floorboards.

▶ Colorful labels of ordinary foodstuffs provide graphic punch, while the humble tin bread box offers useful storage.

▼ This kitchen island was topped with a chopping block to expand usable workspace.

an accent color or two, often some version of red, blue, or green. I concentrate on adding objects and fabrics that feature one of my accent colors. Accent colors might appear in seat cushions, throw rugs, window treatments, pottery, or even fruit or artwork. The judicious use of accent color should be a subtle thing, making a room instantly warm, comforting, and welcoming.

◀ A white expanse is punctuated with the primary colors of these tin sap buckets, which are sometimes found in rural flea markets. They can be used as letter holders, vases or decorative items.

▼ A primitive cabinet left in its original green coat and a winsome pig are sure signs of country.

Look Out—Windows

I am definitely in the "less is more" camp when it comes to window treatments, particularly in kitchens. The Wilken house kitchen window wears a pair of exterior shutters inside—a simple alternative to curtains or fabric shades. The curtains in the Mohn Road kitchen are abbreviated, café style, since the window frames have a bit of architectural interest, and I don't want to cover them completely. Given the lush, rural scenery available to diners in the Jeffersonville kitchen, I kept the window dressing to a minimum: simple, white blinds rolled high.

Gather 'Round the Table—
Furniture and Appliances

Kitchen furniture and appliances can be fun. The chances of my purchasing a brand-new kitchen table with matching chairs are about as remote as the sun failing to rise in the morning. With measurements in tow, I scour flea markets in search of the perfect kitchen table. Whether reproduction Chippendale or harvest farm, my table must be sturdy and cheap. If it is at least

▼ Exterior shutters used indoors create a unique window treatment.

fifty years old, made of strong wood, or enamel-topped, chances are the table will offer style and comfort. The same goes for kitchen chairs. Find only two chairs but require six? I say buy the two, and look for additional chairs as you go. They don't even have to match. Paint them all white and you'll end up with an interesting family to group around the table. Even ordinary chairs are readily dressed up with a coat of white paint. Minimum criteria? Comfort, stability, economy.

I love the look of vintage appliances. There is a certain serviceable enormity in a Magic Chef stove, with its expansive surfaces and enameled durability. These behemoths were truly the

▶ Kitchens are natural gathering places; encourage this activity with plenty of comfortable seating and light.

A Hidden Treasure

I'm always on the lookout for paintings—landscapes are a favorite—to add a swath of color, plus a little dimension, to my predominantly white walls. Whether the artwork is old or new, signed or unsigned, if you collect out of love, you'll never be sorry (see photo on right).

warming, nurturing centers of the rural farmhouse, from which all life and activity seemed to spring. Although many vintage stoves can be used efficiently, I covet them for the color, style, and design implications they impose, and impose they do, as stalwart reminders of kitchens past. The magnificent Magic Chef in the Jeffersonville kitchen holds court while offering infinite storage and an acre of workspace. But nor can I overlook contemporary needs: In the D.C. kitchen a microwave was embedded in the wall, and a

stacked washer and dryer lurk behind a "false" door in the bead-board paneling. Hiding the modern appliances allowed the kitchen to retain a charming country look.

Since storage figures prominently as one of my requirements for home comfort, I've already discussed the need for cabinets and stand-alone shelving. Sideboards, kitchen

▶ A hutch stocked with items both useful and pretty. Don't fear mixing collections of different vintages: here a 1950s coffeepot resides happily with crockery from other periods.

▼ Note the microwave cleverly embedded in the bead board in this city kitchen with a country heart.

▼ A good way to show off country crockery is in this ingenious plate rack.

hutches, corner cupboards, and plain old bookcases also make for excellent storage caches in country kitchens. You can paint these white or leave them as they are, in all their peeling, lived-in glory. Again, remove the doors to expose interesting crockery or add a door, as I did in the Wilken kitchen. I "finished" the opening of a quite ordinary shelf with a

▲ A collection of salt and pepper shakers and covered dishes in the form of barnyard fowl adds a dash of color to a predominantly white décor.

primitive screen door, creating a giant cabinet redolent of the pie safes of earlier times. Filled with the colorful packaging of basic kitchen staples, my contemporary pie safe makes for an organized pantry (see page 32).

Collective Creativity

Collections are natural for a kitchen. Whether you collect American pottery or pink Depression glass, a small gathering of objects creates visual interest. Wood-handled stainless-steel utensils amassed in a ceramic pitcher are handy and appealing. If your accent color is red, why not arrange a farmyard of salt and pepper roosters, covered-bowl hens, and fowl-inspired ceramics?

Don't forget to use artwork in the kitchen. You can pull in your accent color in the blue skies of a landscape painting or the green lettering of old signage or advertising. Artwork is whatever appeals to your eye, so trust your vision. I find old signs and primitive, flea market paintings particularly charming.

Quick Fixes

- Liberate cabinets of doors to expose china collections.

- Cluster a family of like-minded objects, say white enamel kitchenware, in an interesting vignette.

- Display humble foodstuffs … if they have colorful or retro labels.

- Adopt those cheap, reproduction chairs and refresh them with white.

- Choose an accent color for a white kitchen and display it in seat cushions, throw rugs, pottery, or flowers.

- Paint the floors high-gloss white or black for instant impact.

▶ Something as simple as a ceramic bowl filled with fruit creates a lovely still life.

Rooms for Lingering—
Living Rooms

Now stir the fire, and close the shutters
fast, let fall the curtains, wheel the sofa
round, and, while the bubbling and
loud-hissing urn throws up a skinny
column . . . so let us welcome peaceful
evening in.
—William Cowper,
The Task

◄ Pale hues and pure cotton fabric ensure
this sofa's looks and comfort. I love the delicate design on the gaming table so much
so that when it's not in use, it functions as
a kind of canvas, folded up and tilted
against the wall beneath the painting.

I grew up in a house in which the living room

was rarely used. All the furniture was new, fussy, or formal, creating the opposite of what the word *living* seems to want to conjure. An unused room has a particular sensibility, hard to dispel, of stilted air, unyielding furniture, and unspoken conversation. Given the ease and accessibility of the living rooms I have created, it is with no small measure of surprise that I recall the significant effort that went into developing the very atmosphere of effortlessness.

Simplicity is a form of restraint, and one must think about and be conscious of it in order to attain it. But simplicity does not mean that you are allowed only one sofa, one table, one chair. One need not live in a barren room to live with simple design. A single sofa plopped front and center before a "media cabinet" does not a compelling living room make. Nor does simplicity require that you reject formal design altogether. What it does mean is that you learn to edit. Some of my favorite objects have classical lines or Gothic styling: wrought-iron porch furniture and heavy garden statuary

A Hidden Treasure

Bird lovers needn't be concerned about my collection of nests; no birds were made homeless. The nests had long been abandoned and were rescued from the rafters of a dilapidated barn, soon to be demolished. I saved them for the pure sense of country and utility they so wonderfully embody.

▶ A chaise lounge covered in cotton damask and layered with pillows provides a cozy corner for reading or napping. Behind the chaise lounge, an exterior cornice, brought indoors, holds a primitive dollhouse.

bearing Greek or Roman flavors can blend interestingly with a plain farm table or heavy cotton gingham. I try to avoid too much of any one thing, be it color or furniture of one period. A room filled solely with mid-century modern pieces may be interesting, though I would find it inaccessible. But a few shapely ceramic table lamps from the 1950s would mix wonderfully with a humble painted dresser. Edit your rooms so that each contains objects that please your eye, furniture that comforts, and colors that are compatible and calming. It is within such rooms that you will find yourself, and your guests, doing a great deal of living.

▼ The 1940s sofa in my Iowa farmhouse living room was a five-dollar flea-market find. Though worn, I feel no need to reupholster it, although a thorough cleaning was necessary. It's not an Oriental but a good, wool print carpet, also from the 1940s. I love the mellow, faded colors.

▲ I dyed the slipcovers on the Wilken Farm sofa myself and love the results: the precise butter-yellow hue that I wanted and a softly washed, relaxed sensibility.

▲ Off-white canvas slipcovers are both comfortable and practical. Add a cashmere throw for a little luxury in an otherwise casual setting.

An Invitation to Sit

The three muses of comfort, economy, and color inform my every move in living room design. The overstuffed, upholstered furniture of the 1930s and '40s cushions weary bones and can often be snapped up at flea markets and garage sales for a song; appeasing both comfort and economy. The pleasantly plump mohair sofa featured in my Iowa farmhouse was a mere five dollars, and I can't help but smile, perhaps a little smugly, when I see its lines reflected in "contemporary" versions. Don't let threadbare

or torn upholstery lead you to reject a piece of furniture. "Good bones" should be what you're after, and a bulbous '30s sofa or a pair of vintage armchairs can be reupholstered or slipcovered to become part of an inviting arrangement.

Check the bottom of upholstered furniture before buying; most important is that springs and stuffing are not bursting forth. When trying to decide which vintage sofa to buy, unzip the seat cushions. Always opt for down-filled over

foam. Foam can bunch up and harden, whereas down—being a natural filler—can be plumped or even added. Always sit or even lie down on furniture before buying. The last muse you want to anger or betray is our maiden of comfort. If the living room is for living, it must be comfortable.

Cover vintage pieces creatively: think out of the box. Humble cotton works on practically any style, as does heavy canvas or blue-and-white–striped ticking. I tend to introduce color and pattern in more stylized houses: elegant stripes, toiles, or plaids take well to classical design. My brand-new modular colonial in Sullivan County, New York, features a striped sofa and two silk-covered armchairs side by side, adding a dash of formality. In the simple farmhouse or country

◀ Who says elegant and rugged can't meet? Filigreed wall sconces, a gilded frame, and a sisal's fancy floral border cohabitate nicely with a rustic coffee table, handmade newel post, and large checked cotton fabric.

▼ Armchairs, side by side and perpendicular to a striped sofa, encourage conversation in my modular home in Sullivan County, New York.

cottage, I stay with off-white canvas slipcovers, which can be taken off and thrown into the washing machine. (Handy if you've got children or pets scrambling about.) In order to get the particular butter-yellow hue I wanted on the sofa in the Wilken house, I dyed it myself. Using galvanized washtubs set up in the backyard, I dyed the body cover first when the dye was the strongest. Next came the cushion covers, which were dyed, then line dried, to create a weathered, two-toned look. Anyone can do this using store-bought dyes. Practice first, using small pieces of fabric of the same material as that of the slipcovers.

Put It There—A Few Words About Furniture Arrangement

Although it's tempting to back up each piece of furniture to a wall, I try to resist. If space permits I angle sofas or chairs, or even plunk a large piece in the middle of the room. The back of a sofa can separate one seating area from another. Loveseats and smaller-scale sofas are easier to arrange. One trick I use frequently is to place a long narrow table against the wall lengthwise. Then I place the back of the sofa against the table, so the table is between the

Furniture Tips

- Resist buying pieces from all one period or the room will appear either "store-bought" or fussy. Mixing pieces you love, of varying periods, will put a stamp of originality—YOURS!—on the room.

- Use furniture where you need it, not where it's "supposed" to be. Place a hutch, sideboard, or dresser in the living room if the look works for you.

- Splurge, if you can, on one truly great piece for the living room. It might be that dreamed-of sofa or amazing pedestal table; live with special things.

- Sprinkle some "leggy" pieces in among the squat ones. Not all the living room furniture should be low-slung: A room filled with boxy armchairs and sofas will feel bottom heavy. A glimpse of "leg" and a little light between floor and furniture will literally give the room a lift.

sofa and the wall. (This only works if the table is as tall as the sofa's back.) A pair of lamps on either end of the table or an interesting collection completes the look.

Mix taller pieces with squat ones. Don't be afraid to fill space vertically with highboys, cabinets, and tall screens. Prop large mirrors or paintings on mid-height furniture to pull the eye up. An entire wall of bookshelves always looks great and provides ample space to display collectibles, not to mention books. If you are using standard bookshelves, the some-assembly-required type that are readily available in home furnishings stores, resist the temptation to display only one. The shelves will have greater impact if they completely fill one plain of space. Even a narrow wall filled end-to-end with two bookshelves will look better than a large expanse of wall with only one.

A Certain Light

We humans are as drawn to light as moths to a flame. Light represents warmth, safety, and control over the unknown. Why so many people give no consideration to light sources when decorating the interiors of their homes is a mystery to me. Even a hanging overhead light in a rented apartment can be draped with fabric, shaded, or replaced altogether. Proper light in the living room is as integral to good living as is comfortable seating. The light in the living room and rooms in which you entertain should be both flattering and useful. Which is not to say that each source of light has to do everything. An assortment of lamps and fixtures should be considered. Large table lamps with white or pale silk or nylon shades with high-wattage bulbs will shed more than enough light for readers and hobbyists. Smaller lamps with colored or glass shades will lend atmosphere but not much light. Use them to create a mood or as night or entry-hall lights. Change bulbs to accommodate usage. Lower-wattage or even pink-tinted bulbs can be used for entertaining. Place numerous lamps of varying sizes about the room. A pair of lamps has a nice symmetry, especially when displayed at either end of a large table or server, but don't be afraid to mix and match. I use overhead light only in the form of vintage chandeliers, and dimmers are a must. Even the simplest of chandeliers can be dressed up with the addition of miniature shades.

Look for interesting lamp bases at thrift stores and flea markets, where many are for sale. Take the base along with you to purchase its shade, which should cover the hardware but not the decorative base.

Pillow Me

Pillows are a simple, economic route to injecting the muses of comfort and color. Since they require smaller pieces of fabric, you might consider splurging on toiles or velvets. Satin ropes, braids, and tassels or any material you normally think too ornate won't appear overdone on pillows. I've used canvas, bits from damaged quilts, or even burlap sacks with folksy, faded lettering. Look for odd pieces of fabric at thrift stores or flea markets to transform into pillows. Choose one accent color and repeat it in stripes, plaids, and solids. Pillows are a fun, unintimidating way to practice newborn sewing and decorating talents. And if the worst happens, then you can simply cover the pillow again.

▼ The muse of economy loves recycling. Here a burlap potato sack is used for pillow fabric.

All the Rest

For the rest of the furnishings in a country living room, I'm a big fan of bringing the outdoors in. Wooden Adirondack and metal lawn chairs, milking stools, and cobblers' benches can take pride of place in a rustic or not-so-rustic living room. If peeling paint or blotches of rust bother you—for me they decidedly do not—paint everything white. Examine the lines and construction of chairs, benches, or stools: anything three-legged, handmade, or crafted from wood or metal before 1950 will probably have design potential. Metal medical cabinets from the 1940s and '50s make great side tables, and a farm bench can stand in for a coffee table. You can even shorten the legs of a table if it could be better used in front of a sofa. Think about what the object was made for and then ask yourself if it could do double duty as something else. Recycled objects ensure an original living room, the antithesis of "keeping up with the Joneses." By purchasing used objects you help the planet, save money, and create a unique setting for family and friends.

Wood Beneath My Feet—Flooring

Wood floors are featured in all my houses. Mostly it's a matter of restoring, sanding, and refinishing what's there, but I'm so keen on wood floors that I'll install one where it doesn't exist. (If you do install a wood floor over cement, be sure to apply wood decking, insulation, and plywood before the finished wood, so the final effort isn't too hard on the feet. I made this error in a room with low ceilings, not wanting to decrease their height further. Without the other layers, the floor was so hard I had to lay down carpet.) Investigate what is under existing floors before deciding what to do. Perfectly beautiful floors may lie just beneath the linoleum or plywood. Check it out.

Home Comforts for a Living Room

- Sumptuous seating for all

- Interesting art or collections

- Side tables that accept a drink

- Comfortable, durable fabrics

- Table lamps; no overhead lighting (except for wonderful chandeliers)

Whether you polyurethane, wax, or varnish wood floors will depend on foot traffic. Flat polyurethane looks good and wears well, especially when the first two layers are semi-gloss. Waxed floors have a natural, warm glow but are a bit harder to maintain. Lack the funds to refinish badly damaged floors? Simply paint, then polyurethane them. White or light gray will brighten a room; even black can work if you want to go with a more formal look.

Area rugs bring warmth to a room and can help organize a floor plan. Natural-fiber sisals (with cloth borders) are great mixers, compatible with most any design or style of

▼ Warm wood, Roman shades, and plump, plaid pillows all lend an air of elegance to the Harlem townhouse living room. The new wood floors were stained in a natural hue.

furnishings. Size the rug to the room so that a nice, healthy border of wood remains. Oriental carpets or kilims (flat weaves) add formality and can also introduce color. Oriental carpets cycle in price, so defy trends and purchase when

prices are low. I find Oriental carpets timeless and am forever on the lookout for older, faded examples. I actually prefer faded and worn carpets to those that are plush and bright, and have found affordable carpets that were frayed or threadbare. A well-placed plant stand or coffee table can hide many sins. Simple country-cottage floors wear braided rugs well, and you can still find these homemade gems quite

▼ A garden bench in the living room? Why not, if you love the weathered patina as much as I do. And speaking of weathered, my "Old Masters" painting is really a beat-up place mat mounted in an old frame.

cheaply in outlying flea markets or estate sales. Think about the color you want to add to the room and look for it in a carpet, or fall in love with a particular carpet and use its existing color as an accent. Since a carpet is a kind of canvas on which the objects in a room are added, choose carefully. The best rule is always: Buy what you love.

Window Dressing

Living room windows often offer the best views from a house or apartment. I frequently leave them free of window treatments if privacy is not at issue; it's wonderful to let in all available light. But when some coverage is desired (fabric and art can be damaged by sunlight) I am consistently ruled by the "less is more" principle. I love the simplicity, economy, and ease of white roller shades. Keep shades in good repair and at the same level in each window, and they will virtually

disappear. To dress windows with a tad more flair, install flat Roman shades in toile or a printed fabric. Finally, a lush, though not low-budget, third option is full-length curtains of muslin, canvas, or linen, that run along an embedded track in the ceiling. I like the fabric to sweep the floor; to my eye curtains cut to the sill or a few inches from the floor appear dated.

A Lifetime of Collecting

What *is* it about collecting? Whether it's the man with a basement full of vintage jazz LPs, the woman with Bakelite bracelets up her arm, or the bottle collector driven to digging through old dumps in search of a prize, human beings seem hardwired to collect. There's something oddly comforting about a collection, a sense of purpose and order tapped when hunting and gathering like-minded objects. The objects arrayed in a collection can also say something about the collector. What one chooses to collect and display can speak to values, trends, what one holds dear. Not to overstate, I find collections revealing, and since one of the most heartwarming aspects of hospitality is the sense that one's host is opening up a bit in order to draw friends near, collections in the home work toward that end. They say, however softly, "Get to know me. Here's something about me." And they offer a simple way for friends, guests, and family to start a conversation. Think about how your collection can create a circle of intimacy when you invite friends and family into your home.

▼ A collection always has a story to tell; what do your books say about you?

◀ Wonderful windows in the Mohn Road house living room called for a tad more formality: curtains in raw silk that "kissed" the floor. (Line the curtains for protection from the sun.)

My collections of paintings, advertising memorabilia, and artifacts has provided the decorating fodder for seven homes. Despite the fact that my attraction to art is based largely on its ability to evoke a sense of timelessness, I purchase many items on a whim. I rarely have to think about a purchase, partly because the market will not bear it—coveted items don't stick around at estate sales and flea markets—and partly because I buy what I love and love is easy to recognize. But the objects themselves must defy trends. Even though I purchase quickly, whimsically, the painting must have staying power. I am drawn to things that have a mythical quality of having been around forever, things that will be here long after I am not. There is a comfort that settles in when one links oneself to objects that endure. These are not objects of fashion or popularity; they are steady and simple and true.

Flea-market paintings are fun to search for and are as inexpensive or costly as you want them to be. Landscapes are a favorite of mine, and whether signed (preferred because a signature *can* increase value) or unsigned (acceptable), simple rural scenes are particularly coveted. Well-executed portraits are getting harder to find, so I snap up all that I discover, framed or not, and often introduce them as "instant ancestors." Ubiquitous flower arrangements and still lifes make an interesting gallery, and even the most primitive beginners' attempts are worthy if they use color and form ingeniously. Some things to look for when buying paintings are older canvases, signed pieces, interesting frames, and paintings in which your accent colors are featured.

Don't restrict your search for wall art to paintings. Advertising, country road signs, and merchandising efforts from days past bring a relaxed sensibility to the living room. Faded paint, rusted metal, or even crumbling corners can't dissuade me: These are artifacts from America's past, and their scars and imperfections tell a proud story. Any piece with lettering or illustrations from a different era can make enigmatic art. Watch for large architectural pieces such as building cornices, columns, and ceramic bas reliefs at flea markets or restoration facilities. Suspended, hung, or propped against a wall, such artifacts bring visual points of interest to your room.

Collections are created one piece at a time. I didn't set out to collect enamelware or art pottery. My first enamelware pitcher was a serendipitous find; I became so intrigued with its color and form that I found myself looking for more. A few trips to flea markets, and a collection was born. See Chapter 10 for more on how to shop.

▶ It was the rough-hewn quality and faded color of the fire surround that attracted me.

Rooms for a Repast—
Dining Rooms

One cannot think well, love well, sleep
well, if one has not dined well.
—Virginia Woolf,
A Room of One's Own

◀ The largest dining room table you can
find ensures everybody a place. In a pinch,
this table could seat twelve. The stove
adds warmth and décor—and set me back
only $100.

Think of a favorite Thanksgiving celebration

from days gone by or conjure one in your mind's eye. What was the setting of this favorite of feasts: On what sort of table did you dine and how was the table set? Maybe there was a creamy damask tablecloth and sparkling goblets on the sideboard. Undoubtedly there was home-cooked food aplenty, perhaps an earthy Zinfandel and, of course, there were wonderful homemade pies. Many Thanksgivings—that most American of

holidays—take place in dining rooms across the country. Dining rooms cast a celebratory mood: familiar, warm, welcoming, and yet they are a touch more formal than the kitchen.

Dining rooms reflect our commitment to good food, conversation, and time well spent with one another; an entire room dedicated to meals with family and friends highlights the value we place on nurturing and social interaction. Does a dining room need to be fancy to impress? Not in my book. What impresses people most is the feeling that care was taken, thought given to their comfort and pleasure. Care and thought might be expressed in tubfuls of flowers, pressed cloth napkins, chilled wine or fresh lemonade, and gleaming silverware. The mere glimpse of a carefully set

A Hidden Treasure

What to do with a garden gate that pulls at your heart strings? Lacking a proper home out of doors, this architectural treasure deserved better than banishment to the garage or cellar. Wrought-iron grillwork, picket fencing, or even an ornamental trellis can be art for the wall (see previous page).

▶ A comfortable nook for late dinners or a game of chess is dressed with gathered curtains that "kiss" the floor.

table whispers to guests upon arrival, "You are welcome here."

If you are lucky enough to have a room in your home dedicated to dining, I say go all the way: decorate and appoint the room as if it existed solely to welcome and serve loved ones and guests. Get the largest table possible and surround it with sturdy and comfortable chairs. Even if you don't have a room relegated to dining, create a dining niche in the living room corner or in an entryway alcove. Guests are bound to feel special if the dining area comfortably accommodates them and reflects the quiet joy with which their presence is greeted.

Delectable Color

Gray, butter yellow, eggshell, and hues of white are the palette of shades from which I draw again and again when painting dining room walls. You can introduce bright color with flowers, china, artwork, collections of pottery, or even food; walls, ceilings, and floor should soothe and offer a neutral canvas. Rejecting bright wall color doesn't necessarily translate to a flat and dull look. In the Iowa farmhouse dining room the pale cream walls are offset by the Nantucket gray trim. Dressing trim in a slightly richer color adds depth and interest. Even using different shades of the same color can create an impact. In my Sullivan County farmhouse, varied hues of white create a sense of depth in a corner cabinet, each of whose compartments was given a different shade of ivory. Although the variation is subtle, the eye detects an interesting complexity.

Experiment with paint chips held side by side and, even better, purchase small quantities of color and sample it on the wall and trim. Paint colors change with the light, wall texture, number of coats, and proximity of other colors. It's best to test colors on the actual wall on which they will appear prior to purchasing large

Home Comforts for a Dining Room

- The biggest table possible
- Comfortable chairs aplenty
- Loads of fresh flowers
- A sideboard (of any make) to display crystal and silver
- Candles and flattering light
- Pale walls and important art
- Some aromatic, homemade dish, lovingly served

quantities of paint or beginning complex jobs. Make sure your sample patch is completely dry and has the correct number of coats before deciding. Inspect it in different levels of light, both natural and artificial, and at different times of the day and night.

Educate yourself about different paint finishes. My choices are nearly always flat or eggshell, as they suggest a refined simplicity and

are quite forgiving on older walls. High-gloss paint is quite reflective and should never be used on walls that aren't in tip-top shape. All of the wall's imperfections will be apparent. High-gloss and semigloss paints are easier to clean. The pigments that give them their gloss help to hold dirt on the surface. Semigloss paints are usually

▼ The red in a distressed sideboard is picked up in the curtains in this dining room.

employed in bathrooms and kitchens, where surfaces are apt to be wiped nearly daily. Again it is wise to test paint before applying it in a room.

Consider using wallpaper in the dining room, particularly if the house has formal lines, high ceilings, or elaborate trim. Stripes, plaids, toiles, or paisleys strike a regal note and add a decorative element to the room in which you welcome guests. Plain-Jane rooms can be given a decorating jolt with paper. Of course wallpaper can be costly. Look for discontinued, remaindered, or even vintage papers, as long as you can get the quantity needed. Vintage papers are exquisite. Make sure the paper is handleable before you buy. Check out online auction sites for vintage papers, but again be cautioned: you will need the proper amount of paper, and it must be in "hangable" condition. Smaller quantities of wallpaper are ideal as a "cover-up" for furniture in need of such. Wallpaper the panels of a screen, the front of a dresser drawer, or even the surface of tables. Apply paper to the flat expanses of the piece and paint the trim a coordinating color. Paper the shelves of a corner cupboard or line the interior of a glass-doored cabinet for extra punch. Old toiles and wonderful florals are exquisite on French or Asian reproduction furniture.

◄ In a predominantly white dining room the trim was treated with taupe. By painting trim a hue slightly different than the walls and carrying that shade throughout the house, a subtle consistency pulls rooms together.

Dress Up the Windows

One place where silk or velvet drapery falling to the floor might be appropriate is in the dining room. Here a little luxury works. Let transparent scrims of linen or raw silk waft in the breeze or transform a coat-of-arms print or smart stripes into Roman shades. Spend a little of the money you've saved on lush fabrics; scout flea markets and buy preowned textiles. Or stay a more traditional course with simple white blinds.

Sparkling windows are a must for any area where guests gather. Wash the windows economically with scrunched up newspapers and a few drops of ammonia in a bucket of water.

Sit, Break Bread, Stay a While—Furnishings

Start with an enormous table. Surround it with bentwoods, ladder backs, slipper chairs, reproduction Louis XIVs, or even handmade stools. Make sure everyone has a place. Give guests elbow room. Can a wonderful meal be far behind? I love long, narrow farmer's tables, zinc-topped assembly-line counters, or round oak pedestals with expansive leaves. I've been known to concoct my own version with ornately carved legs and discarded lumber. My Iowa dining room features a long table crafted out of wonderful planks from an ancient barn. Make sure that it's sturdy and at just the right height, and your dining room table will serve the hungry and the hobbyists, the jigsaw puzzlers and the late-night homework preparers.

The last thing I would ever purchase is a dining room set. I love serendipity, so part of the joy in setting up a dining room is the hunt for dining room chairs. Sometimes I search for members of a common if not identical family: reproduction King Louis, 1950s chrome, countrified ladder back. Other gatherings have been utterly haphazard: a bentwood here, a milking stool there. Match them if you want, but don't let contrasts scare you. Pull up a slipper chair to mix with the wooden armchairs. A jumble of large, upholstered armchairs circling a round, pedestal table is inviting; just make sure the chairs are high enough for comfortable dining. Some fine day you can cover all your dining room chairs in canvas if symmetry is what you desire. But right now, please the muses of comfort and economy. If all your chairs are hardwood, you may want to cover them with cushions.

Hidden Treasures

◀ Comfortable slipper chairs were used in the dining room of my Harlem townhouse.

▼ What a perfect sideboard a hutch can make. The table was handmade from salvaged barn planks; the legs were from a 1940s kitchen table.

Resist the urge to place flowers in an ordinary vase. Think enameled coffeepots, colorfully labeled cans, old milk bottles, or even olive oil tins. Place glass jars inside tin or metal containers to keep the rust away (see below).

Take a copy of one of the most beloved paintings ever created, place it in an antique frame, and give it center stage. Let the conversation begin (see left).

A sideboard in the dining room makes sense. It is a waiting area for courses yet to be served, a holder of bouquets, a bearer of fruit, a gallery for your collections. Water pitchers and ice buckets perch there, as could an entire bar, if you are of such a mind. Of course what becomes your sideboard needn't have started life as such. An actual sideboard, separated from its mates, will work, but so will a chest of drawers, a corner cabinet, counters from factories or the long-gone five-and-dime. Any piece of furniture with an expansive top, tiers of drawers, or compartments or shelving can house the workings of the dining room. An ornate highboy or low-slung oak dresser will serve equally, and if the wood is too dark or the finish damaged, by now you know my mantra: paint it white! I am not above dressing up a primitive piece through an exchange of hardware and a coat of paint. Even plain-Jane shelving, an unpedigreed counter, or a hutch intended for a country kitchen can make an appearance in the dining room.

Lighting

Chandeliers were made for dining rooms. Don't be afraid to mix ornate fixtures with simple surroundings or vice versa. Simple varieties look great dressed up in miniature shades. A table lamp with a fabric-covered shade is attractive on a sideboard, particularly when low-wattage bulbs and warm-colored materials are used. Cover shades in red silk or orange velvet for a soft yet dramatic look. Don't forget candles. A mismatched group of candlesticks of varying heights and compositions on a sideboard or as a centerpiece is sure to make a meal a little more special.

▶ Even the simplest of chandeliers looks special gussied up with tiny, pleated shades.

Art and Collectibles

I'll never forget the rural scene depicted in an ornately framed etching that hung on my family's dining room wall. It brought a European field during harvest time meticulously to life. Working in babushkas and straw hats was a family of farmers, a multigenerational mowing and gathering and baling of hay. Since nearly every

▼ The cabinet's classical lines are echoed in the column beside it.

A Hidden Treasure

Perfection can be boring. Even though this small statue is broken, what's left is still wonderfully decorative. The broken bits of most objects or artifacts can be hidden from view or even enjoyed for the stories they give rise to.

age group was represented, my family spent many hours of dinnertime conversation matching up the characters in the drawing to members of our own clan. I was forever the blond-haired

◀ An English-style cabinet, originally found in dark wood, was given a fresh coat of white. Period chairs were left unpainted to mix up the look.

▼ Don't keep crisp vintage linen and the "family" silver hidden away, display it whether you use it or not.

boy in short pants, even on return visits. Such is the power of art to connect the viewer to the narrative within. Dining rooms are a great place to display art and start conversations. I save some of my favorite landscape paintings for the dining room walls since I find them both relaxing and thought provoking. Artwork hung on dining room walls will eventually claim the

▼ Collections of enamelware and seltzer bottles fill a dining room.

attention of diners. Collect what pleases you and let the conversations begin.

Gather objects in the dining room both useful and pretty. Search flea markets for fanciful silver-plate trays or salt and pepper shakers, large china pitchers, or enamelware. Don't be afraid to mix and match crystal, silverware, china, or linen. Collect candlesticks of varying heights and materials and group them at one end of the sideboard. Line up colorful seltzer bottles or wonderful weathered terra-cotta pottery. Even the most humble objects create an impact when collected and displayed en masse. Consider a collection of regional

▼ Create a dining nook with a round table dressed up in a toile cloth.

Rooms for a Repast

objects for the dining room, a sure bet for creating conversation. Vintage sporting goods—think wooden skis or snowshoes if you're in snow country—or old glass bottles stamped with regional brands. Tin buckets or watering cans make tremendous vases, particularly when grouped. Prop up a giant mirror on the sideboard for the reflection of crystal, candlelight, and smiling faces.

▼ A wood-burning fire, candlelight, and a good, hearty meal . . . can a pleasant evening be far behind?

Rooms to Dream In—
Bedrooms

What a haven of rest and security is one's own room!
—*The Duchess,* Molly Bawn

◀ The muses of color and comfort come together in the bedroom of my modular home in Sullivan County, New York.

If kitchens are where we gather, bedrooms

are where we retire. The job, the world, the news of the day can all be set aside by closing the door and entering a refuge of creature comforts and thoughtful appointments. We spend nearly a third of our lifetime asleep; if so, how important it is to create a room in which

Home Comforts for a Bedroom

- A comfortable bed

- Fresh bedclothes of natural fibers

- Calm, restful art

- Good reading light

- Handy bedside table

- Ample storage

sleep, and everything that restores us, is easily had. Nowhere do the muses of color and comfort come more to play than in the bedrooms I design. Exuberant color, provocative art, and boisterous collections are left for the more public rooms where conversation and wakefulness are encouraged; in the bedroom I seek quiet, soporific color, ample bedding in comfort-worn textures, and a pared-down sensibility when it comes to objects and furnishings. Computers, telephones, televisions, and the like can chatter away in dens, kitchens, and family rooms; the bedroom is where human beings recharge, restore, and relax their way into another day.

▶ The lilac that freshens this master bedroom's walls is repeated in the antique quilt. Brilliantly hued bottles on the mantel add to the impact.

A Calm Neutrality—Color

It is important to evoke a calm, meditative air in the bedroom, and neutral wall color is one way to do it. Hues of off white, putties, and cream are featured in many of my bedrooms. One combination I find quite restful is in the Wilken Farm house: the ceilings, floorboards, and window frames are white and the walls ecru. The two colors work well to freshen bead-board walls and ceilings, and crisp white paint salvages the badly damaged floors. Neutrals provide a wonderful foil for more colorful linens and artwork. That's not to say I reject color totally. The Harlem townhouse bedroom was treated to a coat of tender lilac, and the master suite in the modular is painted in hues of slate blue and ivory. Use color carefully in bedrooms; you don't want to disrupt.

▼ Warm wood floors, slate-blue walls, and a few pieces of dark furniture create a period feel in the master bedroom of a brand-new house.

Floor Covering

A Hidden Treasure

A vintage radiator retrofitted for modern use evokes a remembrance of things past in a newly constructed home (see photo at left).

Bedroom floors can live without covering if they receive little traffic and if the wood is in good shape. Because my older homes often feature tiny bedrooms, I like to brighten them, and nothing does so as instantly as white paint. If floors do require covering, braided rugs or sisals work well.

▼ A 1940s braided rug and wood floors add to the rustic feeling of this rural retreat.

▼ Or paint floors gray and leave them bare.

Make Your Bed!—Linens

One of the little things that make a room memorable is a bed lavished in wonderful linens. Layers of color and texture, and natural fibers create a beautiful, luxurious bed. I always choose 100-percent cotton or linen when purchasing sheets and pillowcases and since 300-plus-thread-count linen can be costly, I don't limit myself to brand new. Antique linens add extraordinary color and texture and need not be prohibitively expensive. Thrift stores have racks and racks of used linen, and with a little time and a judicious eye, you will come away with cotton sheets; light, summery coverlets; and embroidered pillowcases. Mix lightly used fabrics with contemporary purchases and layer interesting textures of chenille, linen, wool, felt, and lace. I've even bought damaged pieces with embroidered edges that could be salvaged and sewn onto something else. Among my favorite bed dressings are quilts, blue and white ticking, and heavy canvas stripe. Stack loads of pillows and always provide an extra throw at the foot, and the bed won't be empty for long. Crisp, clean linen is always irresistible.

Bedsteads—Head and Foot Boards

A decorative bedstead anchors a room and imparts a sense of timelessness and stability. A mattress and box spring without some sort of decorative frame reminds me of roommates and irresponsibility: fine for then, not for now. Nothing is quite so regal and self-affirming as sleeping in a high, noble bed. Make a commitment to provide a stately frame, quality mattress, and freshly laundered linen.

◀ The small ceramic lamp and bedside dresser were both foraged at flea markets.

▼ Antique bedsteads are well represented in my houses. They pull their weight in a rural farmhouse (below) or an urban pied-à-terre (at right).

It is money and time well spent.

I love searching for antique bedsteads. Flea markets, used-furniture stores, garage sales, and antique shops have all been the source of unique finds. Iron, brass, metal, and four-poster styles are all represented in the bedrooms of my country homes. I have sanded some, painted others, and let many a bedstead be. Rust and peeling flakes don't bother me, but if so you, then paint. My preference is to purchase the entire bed: headboards, footboards and rails. Although rails are replaceable, it's sometimes tricky getting the right length and fit. It is also handy to have standard double and twin

mattress measurements with you in order to determine whether the frame in question will require a custom mattress. Before purchasing the frame, have the seller put it together. I once drove all the way home with the wrong rails. You'll also want to check out the stability of the frame, though bear in mind that the mattress will add stabilizing weight.

If you must have a queen- or king-size mattress, you will be unable to locate an antique frame. There are wonderful reproductions available but most are costly. One alternative is to construct a properly sized headboard from an architecturally interesting object, such as iron grating or, as I did, a white picket fence. Headboards can also be mounted on the wall, creating visual impact with the bed frame pushed up against it. Two twin headboards are about the same width as a king-size mattress; ostensibly, they could be joined side by side to form one long headboard.

▼ Here's the bedstead I constructed from a picket fence. It's quite rustic, but it works, don't you think?

Art

An old American print hung above the bed I slept in at my grandmother's house. A lone wolf on a knoll bayed at the moon. Thoughts of the wild and of Jack London and my own dog at home flitted through my mind as I drifted off to sleep. Images of pleasant rural scenes, gently sailing boats, and portraits of "ancestors," faux or not, may ensure a calm and restorative sleep. Most of the paintings hanging in the bedrooms of my houses were flea-market purchases of a few dollars. Hang a picture or two and give yourself and loved ones something to dream about.

Other Furnishings

A bedside table is a must: alarm clocks, table lamps and a glass of water all need their perch. Older bedsteads with mattress and box spring will mean a bed that is higher than usual from the floor. The accompanying table should be almost as tall as the top of the mattress, therefore standard bedside tables may be too low. Think creatively: use a medical cabinet or even a stack of old leather suitcases. A wrought-iron plant stand would make a charming nightstand if the surface is large enough to accommodate your needs. If you are unable to fit a table next to the

▲ Fresh flowers on the bedside table provide a small delight.

bedside, be sure to affix a wall lamp.

As far as storage goes, steamer trunks and leather valises provide ample space for blankets, linens, and sweaters. Line the cases with cedar strips to mothproof. In most of my bedrooms you'll find a tall chest of drawers. Any dark wood chest built before the 1960s has potential. I paint them white if the wood or veneer is damaged, and more often than not I'll exchange the hardware for older, glass versions picked up at flea markets.

▶ Some might paint this distressed bureau, but I love it in all its peeling glory.

▼ Steamer trunks look terrific and expand a bedroom's storage.

Screens

Paneled room dividers or screens come from an earlier time when a trip to the bathroom otherwise meant a trek to an outhouse, and the lack of running water meant a pitcher and basin in the room one slept in. Screens provided privacy for changing clothes as there were often more than one family member to a bed. They were quite helpful in extending the use of the room.

I find screens just as useful today albeit for other purposes. They can hide a multitude of sins, from overflowing laundry baskets to cardboard boxes and sporting goods. Make a radiator disappear, hide the ugly pipes in the bathroom, or place one in front of an electrical outlet with its explosion of cords. If you don't like the look of a television in the bedroom, use a screen.

Flexible as far as size and color, screens adapt readily to any design sensibility. Fold one

A Hidden Treasure

Former medical or dentistry cabinets provide additional storage and streamlined appeal. Metal furnishings can be stripped or painted to suit aesthetic needs.

▲ Reading material and towels bid guests a fond welcome while pillows clad in red-striped ticking break through the sterility of white.

in half or thirds to make it smaller; paint it, paper it, or add a collage or fabric to make it fit your particular décor. Look for sturdy, wood-framed screens at flea markets and don't be turned off by those whose panels have seen better days. Covered with vintage wallpaper or painted brightly, the screen will be transformed.

Stay the Night—Guest Rooms

The necessity of fresh, clean linen in a guest room can never be overstated. An extra blanket, a strong reading light and a proffered glass of water are de rigueur. Place a bench or trunk at the foot of the bed to accommodate luggage. Have an upholstered chair available so that your guest can unwind comfortably and have a moment alone. Loads of fresh flowers, whether in fancy vases or humble jars are a universally understood sign of welcome. Some light bedtime reading, be it local history or a current magazine, should be stacked by the bedside. Wood or padded hangers are a nice touch, and a bedroom door that can be fully closed is a must. Create the atmosphere of a suite. A guest should feel a sense of comfort, privacy, and welcome, and a little time and care to the room's appointments will ensure exactly that.

Quick Fixes for Bedrooms

- Choose calming, neutral colors for the walls.

- Flowers in bedrooms show attention to detail.

- Display a freshly made bed with wonderful linens.

- Collect inexpensive flea-market paintings (try 1950s paint-by-number!) for the wall.

- Keep tableside clutter to a minimum by installing a wall sconce.

- Place a salvaged iron grate or piece of architectural molding on the wall for an instant headboard.

◄ The "suitelike" atmosphere in this bedroom is enhanced by the inclusion of an armchair covered in crisp striped fabric. Note the two heart-shaped chairs at the foot of the bed taking the place of more predictable bedroom furniture.

Kids' Rooms

Involve your children in the design process. Perhaps they can choose the accent color of the bedclothes or a collectible to display. Small, handmade quilts look marvelous framed and hung in a baby's room. Twin-size bedsteads are perfect for kids' rooms, and easy to find at thrift stores and flea markets. Don't forget a bedside table light to encourage your child to read. Trunks and old wooden shipping cartons with lettering make great toy boxes. (Remember safety first: Check for sharp corners, splinters, and nails, and that trunks can be opened from the inside.)

▶ Pastels in wall color and bed linen make this child's room the perfect sanctuary.

▼ A bedroom edited with an expert eye: calm, neutral colors and lots of dark wood.

▼ Notice the textural differences in this bedroom. Rough brick, smooth wood, and jagged fencing add layers of interest.

A Retreat—
Bathrooms

Retreat . . . to the only existing privacy,
the only place one is permitted to be
unquestionably alone, the lavatory.
—Margaret Laurence,
Winter's Tales

◀ Relax after the bath . . . in an armchair
upholstered in terry cloth. Another
way to fly in the face of tradition is to
leave some of the wood exposed in an
otherwise white bathroom.

95

Luxury can be simple.

The mere glimpse of a stout, claw-footed tub bodes its own special allure: the wonderful crash of water filling the vessel, room enough

Home Comforts for a Bathroom

- Sparkling-clean fixtures in white, white, white

- A tub large enough to soak in

- Mounds of freshly laundered towels

- Faucets and stoppers that work and a good showerhead

- All chrome fixtures; no gold or brass

- Thick cotton rugs to protect your bare feet from those cold tiles

- Sufficient storage

for you to sprawl with a cloudful of bubbles, and finally, a lingering soak up to your chin. Enhance the feeling with an ample supply of lush, terry towels standing by on a vintage chair, and don't forget scented candles and an enormous bouquet of wildflowers.

Many of the bathrooms in the houses I purchased were renovated in the 1960s, which translates to pink built-in tubs and miles of turquoise tile. Since my preference for bathroom fixtures is solidly in the white and traditionally styled camp, these colorful references to days gone by have to go. Tempered as I am by considerations of cost and design, I am unlikely to jump on the "power" bathrooms of the day, all decked out in sunken Jacuzzis and his-and-her sinks. These are simple farmhouses being

▶ I keep small country bathrooms simple . . . and pure white.

renovated, not megamansions, and I am dedicated to restoring the spirit of simplicity with which they were conceived and constructed. The bathrooms in country homes should not scream renovation; comfort, utility, and simplicity are the watchwords of the day.

Floor Me

Believe it or not, my preference for wood floors carries into the bathroom. Ceramic tile is a fairly recent phenomenon, and houses built in the late nineteenth and early twentieth century can look overly processed when decked out in modern materials. High-gloss enamel deck paint works well on wooden floors in bathrooms, but the prep work is all important. All surface paint, epoxy, and dust must be removed before the requisite three coats of paint can be applied. Polyurethane provides an extra layer of protection but may yellow the surface, so only apply it if you like the glossy look.

When ceramic tile is unavoidable in the bathroom, I use standard white 4-by-4-inch squares for reasons of economy. Of course exquisite marbles, composites, cast concrete, and handmade terra-cotta tiles are used in many of today's renovations . . . at a price. I steadfastly advise simplicity even if there is money to be spent: white or natural hues, flat finishes, and traditional or classical design. The bathroom should feel relaxed, not overwrought.

◀ A vintage pedestal sink and new (although traditional) toilet in classic white.

Wall-to-Wall White

Wainscoting figures prominently in my bathrooms, particularly if a claw-foot tub exists or has been installed. Surrounding a stand-alone tub, wainscoting brings a period feel and warmth that ceramic tile lacks. That being said, I can't recommend wainscoting for a bathroom that is used everyday or one in which a built-in cast-iron tub exists. Tile performs well where water is concerned, and the routine splash back from a shower or built-in will quickly damage wood or plaster walls. Wainscoting looks great but is only recommended for weekend homes or ones in which the claw-foot tub is set back from the wall. I love the look of large, white subway (6-by-3-inch) tiles for bathroom walls, but these are considerably more expensive than the 4-by-4-inch version. Avoid pastel-colored border tiles, which date quickly. White is the classic color of choice for bathroom walls, fixtures, and tiles.

Rub-A-Dub-Dub—Sinks, Tubs, Toilets

Traditionalist that I am, claw-foot tubs and pedestal sinks regularly appear in my bathrooms. I love them so much that I'm willing to give up the convenience and storage advantages of fixtures in more modern designs. I am loath to allow a vanity sink, with its undersized water capacity and plywood cabinet to maintain residence in any bathroom of mine. Damn under-the-sink storage! A pedestal sink with its poollike vessel and regal column is a beauty to behold. Sacrificing the convenience of a contemporary sink, I'll opt for dealing with the hot and cold double spigots of a period piece. If you absolutely must have the hot and cold water ushering from one spigot, there are marvelous reproduction pedestals available. What you give up, in the cause of beauty, is storage space below.

Cleopatra is said to have bathed in milk in anticipation of her romantic trysts; if her bathtub was of the claw-foot variety what a lot of milk that would have taken. Tall, curvaceous, leonine-footed period tubs project a stately bearing in any bathroom and provide the most luxurious of retreats. I love to wainscot the bathroom and set the tub out from the wall, featuring it as if it were a treasured piece of furniture. Many late-nineteenth-century homes were equipped with claw-foot tubs, which are also easily obtained at flea markets and vintage appliance and fixture stores. Try to find a tub in relatively good condition, as reglazing is expensive and hard-to-find repair work. A few chips here or there don't bother me if the lines of the tub are artful. Be advised that older tubs may contain lead or other toxins and are unsafe in homes with babies and small children.

Committed as I am to refurbishing period fixtures, I draw the line at commodes. Go for a new toilet in a traditional style and buy only white.

Reject newfangled low-slung or high-style versions. New toilets are practical, work well, and can be easily repaired. Opt for the traditional tank-separated-from-bowl design, and your only decision will be bowl shape. A round bowl will work better if you're tight on space; an oval bowl is longer.

Fixtures

Most of the faucets, handles, and fittings in older bathrooms have to be replaced. Since hot- and cold-water taps, spigots, and the lot are things that you need to count on, new fixtures have the advantage. (A repairperson may gripe that older fittings are hard to fix and that parts are not easily had.) I always choose chrome-finished fixtures, never gold-toned or brass. The only exception is if vintage fixtures are intact and in good repair and are wed design-wise to an existing sink or tub. Purchase the best reproduction fittings you can afford since bathroom hardware is visible, used repeatedly, and needs to be of relatively good quality. Traditional styles, complete with porcelain inlays, are available at nearly all home-renovation outlets.

Claw-foot tubs require special hardware, and in order to maintain the period look and feel, you should splurge on top-grade materials and insist on proper installation. A beautiful

claw-foot tub cries out for porcelain-capped hot- and cold-water taps, a traditional gooseneck faucet, and an oversized, sunflower-shaped showerhead. All of the piping, from the hot and cold intake to the drain, is exposed and must therefore be of high quality. Don't forget to factor in the shower-curtain ring, which must mimic the piping and must be attached by like-minded bars to the wall or ceiling. A claw-foot tub, reconfigured with high-grade materials for use as a shower, will be a splurge well worth the expenditure. One low-cost alternative, perhaps bearable if one is converting a vacation home, is to use the tub only for bathing, thus saving the additional cost of shower-curtain hardware. (You could install a rustic, out-of-doors shower for summer use.)

What if you find yourself in a bathroom renovated in the 1960s, replete with pink, built-in cast-iron tub and far few funds to renovate? Install a hospital-style track on the ceiling above the tub and hang a dramatic black-and-white toile fabric around the tub from floor to ceiling, completely encasing it. You'll need a plastic shower liner of course, which will be completely invisible as will be the pesky pink tub. You could even cover that troublesome vanity in the same wonderful toile. Black and white works with any color, and your only expense will be installing the ceiling track and the fabric.

Mirrors, Medicine Cabinets, and Storage

One of my favorite quests is the hunt for the perfect medicine cabinet. Flea markets and garage sales are good pickings for the distressed mirrors and wall-mounted cabinets that didn't make it through others' renovations. I like cabinets with a certain patina of use that don't necessarily need to be painted. Of course you need to be mindful of lead-based paints. Always remove bits of flaking old paint by sanding and replace painted shelves with glass ones, which are easily acquired at hardware stores.

Try hanging an ornate mirror in lieu of a cabinet for a simple, streamlined look. Desilvering, blips, and bubbles in mirrors just make them more interesting in my opinion, but if clarity is a problem, you can always install a retractable, double-sided mirror on the wall for utility.

▶ A diminutive wall sink and other fixtures turn a closet into a much-needed bathroom.

Recapture the storage space lost beneath the pedestal sink by adding a cabinet, dresser, or hoosier-style hutch in the bathroom, space permitting of course. Towels can be rolled and stacked on cabinet shelves or placed in giant baskets.

Good Light

Simple, good light is a bathroom must. I use vintage fixtures when possible, and when not, I purchase good reproductions from the home-renovation store. Basic porcelain wall sconces with chain pulls are readily available at flea markets and are so simply constructed as to continue to work well. Flat, glass, ceiling-mounted globes from the 1940s let through all available light and provide the overhead necessary for the bath. I love chandeliers, especially those sparkly French vintage numbers but will consider them only for the powder room. Make sure to install bulbs with enough wattage for early morning ablutions.

Quick Fixes

- Hide an ugly built-in tub with a floor-to-ceiling shower curtain.

- Paint and decorate using light airy color for a fresh, calm cohesiveness.

- Cover an offensive vanity in the same fabric as the shower curtain.

- Resolve to take only baths thus doing away with a shower curtain for the claw-footed tub.

- Discard the characterless built-in cabinet and hang an ornate mirror in its stead.

White Is a Color

I rarely deviate from white in the bathroom unless it is to succumb to a slightly darker hue, such as ivory or eggshell, for the trim. White just works in the bath; it is cool, clean, and calming. Avoid frivolous color as it can quickly date the look of the bathroom. Along with walls of white, I stick to simple, white roller shades rather than curtains, since there are times when I seek all available light, and shades can be raised completely.

Wish List

In one of the homes I remodeled in upstate New York, I put practicality aside and lived large. I used a smallish bedroom to make a giant master bath. A pristine claw-foot tub was placed front and center, creating a kind of refuge cum sitting room strictly geared toward adults. Adding an overstuffed chair covered in white terry cloth and a matching ottoman, my sanctuary was complete. I could soak, luxuriate, read, and drowse. A fainting couch or old iron daybed would also work here.

▶ This all purpose medical cart can be used as a baby changing table, hold towels & toiletries, or be wheeled into the living room & used as a bar during parties.

Creating a mood—
Entries, Staircases, and Other Transitional Spaces

Every door has its own key.
—Proverb from Swahili,
Gerd de Ley,
African Proverbs

◀ The entryway in my modular home sets the tone for the relaxed yet stately space that follows.

High on the wall of the entryway

in my grandfather's house in the country was an absurdly long hat rack made entirely of the hooves and antlers of—what I thought to be— terribly unfortunate deer. The hooves pointed upward so as to hold hats. The antlers, which were more like prongs than full racks, were interspersed among the hooves. More than one deer had sacrificed his extremities for the curious device. My grandfather never owned up to having shot the deer, whose grotesque remains lingered there for years, holding the same unused items: a moth-eaten bowler I'd never seen anybody wear; clusters of canes, broken umbrellas, and dog leashes no one could ever explain to me as my grandparents never had dogs; and the worn brown fedora my grandmother donned to fetch the mail when it rained.

Since entryways are a transitional space from the outside in, they give visitors an inkling of what's to follow. And because entryways are spaces in which we tend not to stay, a little daring in terms of décor might just be called for. No, that doesn't mean the heads of hunted animals. But take a risk. Make an impression.

Think of your foyer as a place to set a tone, to create anticipation and curiosity in the minds of arriving guests. Concoct a zone, an entry point, a portal of intrigue that folks long to enter. Make it simple and white and austere or drench it with color and crowd it with collections; but at least do this: create a mood and give a hint of what's to come. Entryways are the ideal place to experiment with one particular look since the commitment made to a particular style is not nearly as frightening as it would be in a larger, more lived-in space. Exaggerate the colors or themes in rooms beyond; the muse of color can get a little bolder here.

▶ The newel post and rail were created by a clever carpenter.

Separate with Color

A simple way to set off an entryway is through color. Even subtle changes in hue, from bright white to eggshell to ivory, can alter a mood. A darker shade that was used for trim in the living room might be smashing in the entryway. Shades too bold for the living room need not be feared in the transitional foyer. Striped or patterned wallpaper adds instant panache and can be economical since only a small quantity is required. If you are in a period house, do a little research into the colors and patterns of the day and try to emulate them in contemporary paper. Check out mural selections at your wallpaper source; wonderful photographic enlargements of autumn leaves or botanicals could fill an entryway with charm.

Are you without a proper entry? If your front door opens directly to the living room or kitchen, create a makeshift entry. Paint or stencil a rectangle on the floor (in front of the door) to create a kind of visual entry space. Then suspend a narrow panel of silk or linen to create a gossamer boundary, or—if space permits—place double-sided bookshelves parallel to the front door to create an island around which traffic must flow. You could also use backless shelves housed with decorative objects to create a barrier that looks smart from both sides.

Home Comforts for an Entryway

- Create a transition space: separate the entryway, through color and pattern, from the adjoining space.

- Light the way: "chandelier" it or place a shapely lamp on a side table.

- Tried-but-true use of a mirror in the entryway provides the opportunity for last-minute inspection. Try a big, drippy baroque mirror, never mind the desilvering.

- Add a small bureau or side table—demilunes work well—to house an oversized tureen or footed tray for keys, change, mail, and such.

- Create an impression with scent: welcome guests with an abundant bouquet, burn a fragrant candle (safely!), or spritz a pleasant floral mist.

- Lay a small area rug for dusty feet; try an oriental, a braided rug, or small grass mat.

- Resist the urge to use the entryway as a dumping ground. Keep it free for passage.

- Provide a trunk, chest, or small dresser to store gloves, hats, and other outdoor accessories.

Light the Way

The simplest of entryways can be dramatically transformed through lighting. Don't settle for the mundane: go crystalline and confectionary, baubly or baroque, or moodily Moroccan. Don't overaccessorize: pair a dripping teardrop chandelier with the simplest of side tables. The drama of lighting can be offset by austerity. Nearly every foraging trip to the flea market uncovers numerous chandeliers. Be sure to look in boxes and under flea market tables since chandeliers are hard to display. Electrifying a chandelier is a simple matter so most vintage models can be made to work. Hanging them requires a relatively inexpensive visit from an electrician or handyman. Suspend an interesting fixture in the foyer for instant pizzazz.

If your foyer is makeshift, or there's no extant ceiling fixture, illuminate the area with a table lamp. A softly lit entry conveys immediate warmth to nighttime guests. A large selection of vintage lamps is always available at house and garage sales. Look for ceramic numbers from the 1960s with comely shapes and lively colors, chrome or wood models from the '50s or art pottery–based examples from the '40s. If the lamp is missing a shade, take the base with you to pick out a new one. (Make sure the shade covers the hardware but not the decorative base.) I am always on the lookout for vintage

▲ An old outdoor fixture—perhaps an exterior lantern—is painted and brought indoors.

shades, as new ones are quite expensive, and the older ones seem better made. Cover torn shades with panels of fabric or lace; the effect is beautiful, particularly when lit.

Up the Down Staircase

Staircases are so appealing to me that I took down a wall in my Sullivan County farmhouse to expose one. I fashioned a newel post and banister from barnyard lumber, shedding light on the staircase and opening up the entry hall. The triangle of bead-board paneling that remained was painted in broad stripes of alternating ivories, grays, and yellows—all colors featured in other rooms. Try lighter colors on the treads of stairs; they seem to give a visual lift. (A tan or beige won't show scuff marks as much as white.) A staircase should be bright and optimistic, not dark and brooding.

Since a staircase offers a swatch of wall, it's a natural for a small gallery of artwork. Small rural scenes or black-and-white photographs work well; hang a collection of pictures rather than one or two large ones. Avoid too many family portraits in public areas; save your photos of loved ones for a bedside table or desk.

Unless you can afford high-quality carpeting and the rails needed to anchor carpet safely, leave the staircase bare. Unless the risers and treads on the staircase are extremely wide, avoid placing items on the treads. Stairways need to be free of accident-causing clutter.

Quick Fixes for Entries, Stairways, and Halls

- Create an entryway where there is none by painting or staining a rectangle on the floor and adding a fabric scrim as a boundary.

- Hang clusters of small paintings or prints. Choose a theme: rural exteriors or black-and-white photos.

- Wallpaper the entry with bold color or pattern.

- Line the entryway with books for an impromptu library.

- Provide a chair as a receptacle for mail or keys or as a place to remove boots.

- Paint a faux floor or try your hand at a mural.

- Hang a long row of wooden pegs for outdoor wear or even some art.

- Experiment with elements of a specific design period in the entryway and see if it fits.

Hallways

Don't ignore the design possibilities that hallways present. Paint the hallway in colors that are brighter than the ones you've used in adjoining rooms. Curate a show of your favorite art on the walls. If your halls are wide enough, line them with books. Make sure passage through hallways is clear and easy, and light the way if it is particularly dark. Line the floor with an Oriental-style runner or grass matting.

Hallways also present an opportunity for risk taking. If you've always wanted to paint a mural or create a graphic pattern on the floor, a hallway could be your practice canvas.

Raised-panel wood covering in a hallway brings a touch of elegance to an otherwise undistinguished area. Although raised paneling can be expensive, the small amount a hallway requires would keep the cost from being prohibitive. Or you could add bead board or wainscoting.

▼ Notice the subtle changes in hue on the bead-board staircase.

▼ A hallway makes an ideal gallery for a collection of paintings, while, in the distance, a still life of white pottery poses.

Watching the World Go By—
From the Porch

There is more to life than increasing its speed.
—Mohandas K. Gandhi

◀ Folding chairs are fine for porch dining. They're easy to move and enhance the carefree atmosphere.

Before television, before air conditioning

and international travel, before cell phones and browsing the Web, Americans sat on their porches. Sometimes they chatted about the day's events, sometimes they sought the coolness of the night air, and sometimes they simply watched the world go by. Porches represent a simpler time, a time when slowing down the inexorable spin of the planet was as easy as squeezing some lemonade or brewing "sun" tea and whiling away the evening in a favorite rocking chair. Conversation came naturally on porches: perhaps the unique structure of the porch—exterior yet sheltered from the elements—encourages people to open up. On a porch the world lies before you, filled with possibility, and yet home lies reassuringly behind, a bulwark of stability. On porches across America recipes have been exchanged, arguments have been reconciled, marriages have been proposed, and dreams have been launched. Whether your porch is a wraparound standout on a fine Victorian, or an 8-foot-by-4-foot terrace in an urban pied-à-terre, think of it as an extension of your living space and as a place to encourage your American dream.

Houses built in the late nineteenth or early twentieth century were built for utility: rooms were small and created with purpose. Bedrooms contained a dresser and a single or double bed; bathrooms were small if they existed at all (remember outhouses?). And kitchens were often the largest room in the house, being, as they were, the center of food preparation and consumption. A porch or sunroom extended valuable living space in the spring, summer, and fall. It was a place to enjoy the outdoors while retaining the comforts of home. Porches were both a necessity and a luxury at the same time.

▶ I wish I had more chairs like this delicious little heart-shaped number that I snatched up at a flea market.

A Porch Sets the Tone

Seen from the road by passersby, offered as the first welcoming embrace to invited guests, porches set the tone of what's to come. Locked in my childhood memories are glimpses of a neighbor's porch, attached to a house whose interior I longed to see yet never did. The porch was reached by a wide set of stairs, and on either end of each tread squatted wonderfully weathered terra-cotta pots cascading with tricolored ivy. Two enormous wicker rockers awaited weary travelers. The floorboards were painted a crisp, military gray, and this, along with the symmetry of each pot and wildness of ivy, filled me with a kind of longing. The porch beckoned to me with a wordless, soothing tranquility. I knew the people who lived in that house valued simplicity and that what was left out was just as important as what was included.

How are you planning to use the porch?

- As a place of transition, merely as passage from the outdoors to the indoors?

- As outdoor seating, a place for drinks and conversation?

- For seasonal dining and entertaining?

- As a container garden, a place to cultivate flowers and herbs?

- Knowing ahead of time how the outdoor space will be used will allow you to focus on appropriate design and furnishings.

If You've Got It, Flaunt It

If you are lucky enough to have an exterior porch, use it. Think of it as an extension of the living space of your home. Porches can be particularly helpful in a small house by adding functional square footage. Since the porch is the point of arrival at any home, it will inform guests of what lies behind. You want your home to be welcoming, comfortable, and stylish, and the place to start is the porch. Think about how the porch will be used before embarking on design.

▶ The front porch of the Jeffersonville house just calls out to passersby, "Come sit and sip a mug of cider."

The Porch as Transition Space

Whether or not you use the porch for anything else, it is intrinsically a transitional space. It takes you and your guests from the outdoors in, bridging the outside world and the domesticity of home. Making that transition a pleasant one tells guests volumes about the way you live and the things you value. Your porch should be attractive, and should include at least a working doorbell and natural-fiber welcome mat for dusty feet. Since less is often more, keep your porch clutter-free and safely off the worst-dressed list.

The Porch as Dining Room

Few things seem as charming or as American as eating out-of-doors. A porch wide enough to accommodate a table and chairs extends your home's dining areas and encourages dinner by candlelight in the night air. Whether it's a small round table for two or a picnic table and benches for six, make it festive by covering it in linen and using real utensils. Grace the table with cut flowers and candles and you'll be transported to a Tuscan ristorante or a sidewalk café in Paris. But this is your home: make it comfortable for family and friends and every invitation extended will be gratefully received.

I couldn't help but notice that when we ate on the front porch at the Mohn Road house in the dog days of July and August, passersby on the road would slow down their vehicles and stare. Were they fascinated by the festive grouping of our friends and family, so comfortably engaged in food and conversation? Were they diverted by the flash of silver, the merry ring of crystal? Had the soft orbs of candlelight mesmerized them from afar? Perhaps it was the entire scene, as carefully put together as any stage production and yet emitting an aura of comfort, hospitality, and cheer. Part of my carefully edited design for Mohn Road included a scrim of mosquito netting surrounding the

Porch Faux Pas

- Spindly, too-thin porch columns are unattractive. The supporting columns that hold up the porch roof should have some heft.

- Avoid displaying nursery plants in the plastic pots and short wire hangers they came in.

- American flags are fine; novelty flags are not.

- Refrain from placing rejected indoor furnishings on the porch.

- Be creative and eschew formal, matching sets of outdoor furniture.

- Do I even have to mention the bucket seats from cars?

- Don't use the porch as a dumping ground for things unwanted.

- Never cover the porch in outdoor carpeting. "Au naturel" is the way to go.

- Those "clever" sayings on welcome mats such as "Go Away" or "I gave at the office" are a big no no.

▶ Cloth napkins add panache to an alfresco meal. The additional seating at the table is a porch swing.

perimeter of the front porch. I embedded hospital-style tracking on the ceiling so the net could be parted or closed. The effect was both simple and powerful. It created an open space for meals that retained a special intimacy. Seen from the road, with candlelight twinkling beyond the scrim, the porch must have seemed a sort of iridescent oasis.

Furnishings for the Porch

Choose wrought-iron tables with glass surfaces, three-legged side tables, and plenty of Adirondack-style chairs. A porch is not a porch without a rocking chair, and for me, the big wicker numbers from coastal resorts are the best. I like the symmetrical look of the same style of chair lined up on the porch, be they Adirondack or rocker, to underscore the ideal that all porch seating is created equal.

If your porch is furnished with hard wooden chairs, be sure to provide comfortable seat cushions covered in blue-and-white

ticking, gingham, or plaid. Don't be afraid to use brighter colors or larger patterns on porch furniture. The expansiveness of the space calls for a little more exuberance.

I love a porch swing, the boxy, wooden kind, which must be chained to beams in the ceiling. (Be sure to find those cross-support beams!) A great place to look for wooden

▼ A transparent scrim creates a "wall" of netting and a magic place for a summer meal.

porch swings is in import/export shops that specialize in furniture from India or Pakistan. Indoor swings are very popular there and make terrific porch swings for savvy Americans. You can also look at flea markets and garage sales for the typically American kind. Load up the swing with pillows covered in the same fabric as that of the seat cushions.

Metal furnishings work well on a porch, be they 1940s lawn chairs, more industrial-type stools, or even medical cabinets acting as storage or side tables. Try not to crowd too many pieces on the porch or use it as a dumping ground for furnishings too tired for the interior. If you wouldn't have it in the house, it probably shouldn't go on the porch. Remember that the porch gives your guests the first impression of your home. Don't greet them with something that you've already rejected as not good enough for the interior.

▶ Large, identical chairs with cushions, a rustic bench, and clean, white trim create a crisp look in this inviting porch.

A Hidden Treasure

Pillows add a homey, inviting touch to the porch, so don't restrict them to the living room. Look for hand-crafted examples at flea markets in felt, cotton, or, canvas (see photo at right).

Plants and Such

Although plants definitely have their place on the porch, I stay away from the ubiquitous store-bought containers of green plastic with wire hangers. I prefer interesting clay cachepots or traditional ones made of terra-cotta. Evergreens and deciduous trees look grand on the porch, but check with an expert to see if they'll survive the confines of a container. Plain wooden planters will always be fashionable because of their simple lines. Flea markets and garage sales are filled with porch-worthy containers. Use a low, wide-mouthed barrel for a colorful mix of flowering plants. Line up cast-concrete flower boxes along the perimeter of the porch and fill them seasonally with peonies, daisies, or swaths of evergreen. Livestock watering troughs make great planters and have a rustic quality. Remember to stock only as many plants on the porch as can be cared for, as there's nothing so discouraging-looking as shriveled or dying greenery.

▶ Good wood chairs painted white work well indoors or out. A tiered garden table adds a dash of formality.

◀ I love a porch swing.

Porch Flooring

Keep the surface of the wood floors on your porch in top-notch shape by freshening them every spring. I use high-gloss deck paint after prepping the surface with an oil-based primer. Use neutral colors in beige, taupe, grays, and tobaccos for this heavily trafficked area. Never put down all-weather carpet on the porch; it is always unattractive. You should be able to walk across the porch in July and feel the floorboards, or at the very most, a braided rug beneath your bare feet. A welcome mat is not objectionable as long as it is made of stiff, natural fiber.

Roof Supports

The columns that support the roof are a decorative aspect of the porch design. I prefer columns with some girth to them. Spindly, thin-armed versions give the impression that the roof will drop in exhaustion at any moment. A country house should look solid and stable, not sad or droopy.

▶ I wouldn't think of using anything but wood in porch rails or latticework. To me, these materials are fundamental to the atmosphere and authenticity of a farmhouse porch.

▼ A certain randomness and lack of symmetry adds to the appeal of this porch.

Railings

Railings around porch perimeters and stairways are a safety as much as a design consideration. Although I prefer the original/antique turned posts and railing, safety codes must be met. Be sure to follow local regulations regarding railing height and material. All stairways, no matter the length, must have a railing. The only sort of porch that does not require a railing is one in which the surface is flat to the ground.

Sun (and Screened) Porches

Consider sunporches as half in/half out of the house. Often rooms that began life as porches, they extend the family living space and provide a great environment for plants. Since they are not usually heated, unlike the interior, they can be retired in the colder months yet used heartily in spring, summer, and fall.

Because they bridge the interior of the home with the out-of-doors, sunrooms can be dressed in causal and comfortable togs. Keep colors and fabrics light and summery, and never weigh down the sunporch with

heavy draperies, wall-to-wall carpeting, or boxy, modular furniture.

The memory of spending summer evenings on a screened-in porch is an indelible one: Crickets and cicadas figured prominently in the soundtrack, and many hot summer nights were spent camped out on aluminum loungers, our sleeping bags unopened.

Home Comforts for Porches

- Light, summery fabrics: think blue and white, canvas and linen.

- Graceful, leggy furniture as opposed to boxy, modular sectionals.

- A divan, fainting couch, or daybed dressed with pillows is irresistible . . . and provides an additional guest room.

- Simple, white roller shades or scrims of linen at the windows temper the sun when need be.

- Loads of fresh, cut flowers in huge white ironstone pitchers.

- An interesting collection: a stack of antique, leather-bound books; an enormous basket of seashells; a yellow mixing bowl of apples.

▶ The ultimate sunporch: the covered armchair, shaded lamps, and dark-wood side table add a dash of formality.

▼ This mudroom is a jumble of interesting artifacts including a slatted bench and loads of terra-cotta pots. Don't be afraid of a little studied messiness.

Mudrooms

Mudrooms were aptly named. Situated as a rear or side entrance from the yard, these small vestibules were the perfect place to shed rain-soaked cloaks and mud-encrusted boots. Treat mudroom floors to the same application of high-gloss deck paint as that of the exterior porch. Provide rows of wooden pegs for outdoor wear and vintage trunks for mittens, hats, and sporting goods. Retain that old cast-iron radiator and place hooks above it for drying damp garments. If you are fortunate enough to have a mudroom, don't treat it as a lowly cousin when it comes to design. Create a vital and interesting transition space.

❧ A Hidden Treasure

The ring of a rotary phone is a charming sound in these days of rampant digital technology. Red or black models can still be found at flea markets and often still work (see previous page).

▲ Pale gray floorboards and a background of green make this sunporch an excellent spot for breakfasting.

Home Comforts for Mudrooms

- Well-protected floors: think high-gloss deck paint or polyurethane.

- Plenty of hooks for winter coats.

- A bench on which to sit to remove footwear.

- Vintage trunks or toy boxes to house winter wear or sporting goods.

- An interesting and stable umbrella stand for bumbershoots and canes.

- If you're using the mudroom as a potting shed, line up rows of vintage terra-cotta pots and display antique gardening tools.

▶ Pine-board storage expands the use of the mudroom.

In Town—
A Country
Sensibility

The city has a face, the country a soul.
—Jacques De Lacretelle,
"*Les Paysages Herites,*"
Idees Dans un Chapeau

◀ In the Harlem townhouse, I've played with traditional "country manor" colors—greens, blues, and greys—and alternated all those shades on the walls behind my bookcase.

A trip to any city garden center

proves the theory that even the most die-hard city dwellers want a little country in their lives. City nurseries offer everything from the indestructible sansevieria to a delicate Japanese maple and bring the possibility of a little greenery, a chance for inhabitants otherwise relegated to taxi-filled avenues and parking regulations to till the soil. And if bringing a potted plant indoors is not enough country for a fix, many cities offer pocket parks, empty lots usurped by hungry, urban farmers, and community gardens, bits of land parceled out to a lucky few. Of course the major city parks are filled with people homesick for a little country. They walk their dogs, run cross-country, bird-watch, picnic, and stargaze. In other words, they try to bring some of the charms of rural living into a decidedly urban environment.

Most people who dwell in large urban centers live in apartments, and apartment living can mean limited space. But that shouldn't mean that city slickers with a little country in their souls have to go without. Bringing a touch

🌿 A Hidden Treasure

Use your bookshelves to display art. Paintings can be hung directly on the case, as shown here, or propped up on shelves (see previous page).

▶ A mantle was added for its decorative panache as well as display possibilities. Where one bloom is pretty, three are disarming.

Usher in some country, feet firmly planted in the city, by minding these "Dos"

- Feature at least one overstuffed piece of furniture covered in heavy cotton canvas, corduroy, striped ticking, or some other durable yet comforting fabric.

- Inject rooms with pale color schemes: think ivories, butter yellows, soft hues of green or gray, mixed with some chunky, dark-wood furniture.

- Infuse a lil' bit of wild with lush greenery, kept in tiptop shape and housed in interesting cachepots.

- Display a collection of objects, but since space is at a premium, make it a unique one and use clever space-saving means for display.

- Bring the outdoors in with a lovely garden sculpture, the more weather-beaten, the better. Place it as a sentry at the end of a long table behind the sofa or on the floor emerging from a sea of live plants. Or have it stand guard at the end of a hallway and light it from above. Heavy stone planters, elongated ones embedded with designs, make wonderful additions to city apartments. Fill them with pots of ivy or use them to reflect seasonal offerings.

- Mix a few modern pieces to give the space a little edge. Choose a Lucite lamp or an art deco cabinet.

- Add a piece of wrought-iron furniture, perhaps a vintage chaise or an ornate chair, and layer it with overstuffed pillows in blue-and-white cotton ticking.

- Place area rugs over wall-to-wall carpet; use a worn Bokhara, flat-weave kilims, or grass-woven sisals.

- Devote one wall in the apartment to books of many widths, heights, and colors, and suddenly you're transported to the library of an Irish country manor in an earlier century.

- Layer vintage linens to create a timeless look: crewelwork pillow cases in the bedroom, lace-edged tablecloths over plain ones on side tables, or pastel-hued hankies gathered in a basket in the bathroom.

- Satisfy the need for a rural view with a large landscape painting or a series of small country scenes.

- Employ a few large architectural pieces in a living or dining room (if you're lucky enough to have one). A leaded window layered over the existing one, a standing column, or even industrial molds or building cornices would make an immediate impact.

▶ Flowering plants, a cement lion, and a green-hued tub coexist happily inside a city abode.

▼ Polished wood floors, white walls and slipcovers, and a pair of rural landscapes keep this breakfast nook streamlined and sleek.

of the heartland to a high-
rise apartment is both possible and fun.
Accompanied by the three muses of color,
comfort, and economy when setting out to
decorate a city apartment will mean that a little
bit of country is sure to follow you home.

Whether I am decorating a weekend
country house or a high-rise in the city, I delete
from my country look anything that is too cute
or fussy or that can't be put to some use other
than merely decorative. Stuffed animals, small
porcelain figurines, and unusable cachepots are
generally banished. Earthenware pots that can
double as vases, tin containers that hold
anything from tea to umbrellas, and chests and
toolboxes that double as storage are welcomed
and given pride of place. In city apartments,
where space is at a premium, objects must pull
their weight.

If country is a state of mind then there's no
better place to prove it than within an urban
dwelling. This doesn't mean that you have to
fill your city apartment with antique farm

◀ Architectural elements with a country pedigree
add textural interest. A leaded window, at left, is
hung above a newel-post lamp. The desk was probably once used in a hotel or post office as a clerk's
workstation.

▶ A mercury vase from the 1920s looks decidedly modern in a city entryway.

implements or pie safes. Obey the muses to bring in a touch of country.

The muse of economy acts as a sort of editor in the design process. A city apartment filled with large country furniture, overly "chintzed," and loaded with collections will seem overcrowded and inappropriate. Carefully chosen pieces that are wonderfully made or representative of the best of what the style or genre has to offer will make the room appear stylish, particularly if the items are well displayed. Think small collections of important objects: three or four lovely samplers expertly framed and hung together or a small selection

▶ Clean lines and bare counters in a pint-sized city kitchen are chic. Poured-cement counters, bead-board cabinets, and a wooden column contribute to the kitchen's urbanity.

Refine Your Country Look by Minding These "Don'ts"

- Resist buying furniture all of one period, whether antique or reproduction; it will appear too fussy. And the old adage that one must choose a common wood is passé. Mix dark and light, soft and hard.

- Say no to a single pattern or color; every-thing clad in gingham will be "precious"; however, a mixture of stripes, solids, and plaids, with one or two unifying colors will marry rural with chic.

- By all means feature a distressed side-board, cabinet, or sets of chairs in "need" of paint; just don't present a roomful of such pieces.

- No silk flowers, fake plants, plastic pots, or stuffed animals, please.

- Do not overcrowd; too much of a good thing is too much of a good thing. Employ space and allow each much-loved object to breathe.

- Avoid reproductions when possible. Vintage pieces are more authentic, better built, and generally cheaper. Genuine country goods can be found in city antique shops, but why not visit an out-of-town flea market or auction and get it for what the dealer would have paid?

- Papering a wall or even the surface of a cabinet or piece of furniture is a great idea, but avoid using vinyl papers or the surface will have a plastic-looking sheen. Wonderful vintage papers are available and although pricey, they introduce the warmth and charm of a different era.

◀ Sepia tones of brown, black, and ivory impart a modern sensibility to a rural or city bedroom.

▶ A few carefully chosen pieces take the limelight in this entry. Note the juxtaposition of styles: an art deco vase, a mirror moderne, and wonderfully embroidered chairs.

▼ A collection of white stoneware marries rural practicality with city style.

of needlepoint footstools grouped beneath a glass-topped coffee table. In an urban setting, artifacts of the past denote a rural simplicity but should be collected and displayed with a smart city edge.

The muse comfort pairs an overstuffed chair with a mismatched ottoman and loads of pillows crafted from vintage fabrics. Too much steel, glass, or an entire room based on the aesthetic of one period are prohibited in order to avoid pretentiousness. In the city, comfort also means freedom from clutter, the ability to move about.

Country visits the city in ivories, butter yellows, pale grays, and blues; there's lilac and both a whispering and more verdant green. Color is the embodiment of country, the very notion of it, and as subtle as it appears in these pages, it is the essential muse in conjuring a country sensibility.

▶ Washed-out blues and pale green make a calming still life.

▼ This "fancy" fireplace screen adds a point of interest to this "plain Jane" 1928 fireplace.

Fabulous Façades—
Exteriors

Simplicity, carried to an extreme,
becomes elegance.
—Jon Franklin,
Writing for Story

◀ The exterior of the Iowa farmhouse in a
dusting of snow. This shot was taken from
the grounds.

At a recent country auction,

one of the furniture handlers fascinated me. Usually powerfully built men clad in the ubiquitous uniform of denim jeans and flannel shirts, furniture handlers are front and center at auctions, moving items to and fro as they come up for bid but rarely uttering a single word. At this particular auction, the handler was a woman. She was in her forties or even fifties but had a muscular build. Hers was the sort of physique born of day-to-day labor, not the gym. Unadorned by makeup, her skin was clear but not young. Crows' feet and the effects of the sun marked her. Her hair was cut short, perhaps by her own hand; hands with strong, tapered fingers and bluntly cut nails, a large turquoise ring the only jewelry. Uncoiffed, untweezed, unbleached, un-botoxed, she seemed happily unfazed by trends or aging.

Simplicity is charm. And less is often more. Much like a woman who dresses for an evening out and removes one accessory before heading out the door, the allure of many a farmhouse façade lies in what is absent: blinding color, vinyl siding, too new brass, plastic shutters, period-altering stucco.

It's said you can't judge a book by its cover, but no matter what anyone claims, there are things to be learned about the occupants of a house by a glance at the home's exterior. Perhaps you can't discover all there is to know, but certain aspects of personality peep through in color, ornaments, and façade. What does the exterior of your home say about you? What would you like it to say?

▶ I wanted the Mohn Road house to be stately yet welcoming. Clearing away low-slung ornamental shrubbery around the perimeter "opened" the house; of course the magnificent trees remained.

If you haven't suspected this by now, I am much more likely to end up the owner of a simple clapboard farmhouse than of an extravagantly bedecked Victorian, which is not to say that a turn-of-the-century turreted piece of gingerbread can't be fabulous, all done up in historically relevant pastels. It's simply not for me. Remember I'm just a poor dirt farmer from Iowa, and a poor dirt farmer I'll always be. And while I happily submit to the twenty-first-century necessities of wireless access and satellite technology, I want my homes to retain an earlier simplicity. And so simplicity is the watchword, whether I'm choosing an exterior color, deciding on window sashes and shutters, or meeting with the landscaper who will finish the yard.

White, Of Course

I have learned two important lessons in my years of choosing color: (1) the color you imagine in your mind's eye will never, ever be realized on a surface; and (2) white always works. As far as the first lesson goes, it's simply very difficult to simulate the color displayed in your mind or even the color on a paint chip. Exterior colors are particularly churlish because of the ebb and flow of natural light. Of course there are paint masters, and I'm not speaking of people who work in paint stores but specialists who will—for a fee—help you choose a paint, test various paints, and even mix and deliver paints to your door, with the added advantage of being able to replicate your color when the time comes. But I like to keep things simple which is why I nearly always heed lesson two and stick with some hue of white, within which color range I consider ivories, pale grays, and even some distant yellows to fall. White is easy and uncomplicated, but it is also the stuff of my dreams and fantasies. It is clean, fresh, and goes with everything. Even the muse of color agrees. How fortunate that the

An Inviting Home

- Clapboard, not vinyl, siding.

- Restraint when it comes to additions, be it a bay window or roof material.

- Color relative to the origin of the house. Remember white always works.

- A less-is-more theory when it comes to the grounds, especially with regard to lawn ornamentation.

- A simple approach to landscaping. Think green grass.

- No plastic ever, whether it be pots, window boxes, latticework or fencing.

- Discrimination when it comes to outbuildings: no aluminum sheds, mobile homes, or disheveled animal coops.

easiest solution is also one that offers such design potential. You can choose white out of cowardice and fear of color (in which case I won't blame you), or you can choose white, secure in your status as a design savant. Either way you won't go wrong. A white house can be trimmed in green or black or gray and can even afford contrasting color on trim or shutter. And subtle changes make wonderful statements: how

smart-looking is a cream-colored house with crisp white trim? The greatest risk I've ever taken with color was using colonial yellow on a two-story clapboard farmhouse, but it worked. (Perhaps it was the authenticity of the yellow— it was historically accurate—or perhaps it was the contrasting green of the surrounding pines.) If you are interested in pursuing color, major paint manufacturers, who offer historical paint collections, can help ensure accuracy on period architecture.

▼ Simple clapboard: I'm always happy to find it as I did in Iowa.

All the Trimmings—
Some Words on Windows

Structures without windows are cheerless things. How else to bring in the light, remind us of weather, view nature or society, and to announce, yes, someone lives here? How often I recall in my youth, passing by a distant house on a winter night, windows aglow, beacons of warmth in the gloom, as I tried to imagine what conversations were made, what meals consumed beyond them.

Many homeowners will one day confront the issue of window replacement. Simplicity is again the watchword when making such a design decision. I try to avoid dressing up a turn-of-the-century farmhouse in the silks and satins of another period. Simple, double-hung windows and what are called "divided light"— individually paned—windows are my two favorites. When possible I keep the original sashes since storm windows and screens can easily be made to fit vintage models. And there's nothing quite like the patina and quality of original glass. (The only pitfall I've found in retaining old windows is that they are smaller than the windows of today.) Resist the temptation to force a bay, bow, or box window into a façade that never would have had one; such an anomaly almost always looks tacked on and inappropriate. Plus, simpler window selections cost less than their grander, gaudier counterparts. (The muse of economy smiles.)

Will Return in the Spring—Shutters

Drive by the coastal homes in New England in late autumn and you will see that many have been shuttered for a long winter nap. There's something comforting about the ritual of putting a summer home to bed for the season, and nothing symbolizes this more than working shutters. Tongue-and-groove shutters that actually work are the most charming, while traditional louver-style are the easiest to reproduce. Simple cottages and one-story cabins look swell in solid-wood shutters with cutouts of moons, stars, or flowers. Try to use the vintage shutters that came with the house, but if they must be replaced, I insist that you use wood and reject

▶ I took what was, for me, a chance and painted my modular colonial a historic yellow. It works, don't you think?

vinyl or plastic. The advantages of vintage shutters are the usual ones of charm and a hand-hewn quality. Good reproductions, however, are easily had and offer easy installation and a precise fit. Shutters present the homeowner with the opportunity to add a second or even third color to the exterior of the house. Evergreen, black, gray, or cream shutters add punch to a crisp white façade. Add sets of stays in scroll or latch design, or even a primitive oversized hook and eye, and the shutters will have a finished look and be ready for winter.

Window Boxes

I love window boxes but use restraint when it comes to choosing them. Nothing too gingerbready, doll-like, or ornate passes muster. I wouldn't think of using plastic, only wood, or very good, basic terra-cotta. I take advantage of the opportunity window boxes present to seasonally alter, however minimally, the exterior of the home. It's wonderful to have something growing come early spring, and tulips do well in boxes, provided they have proper drainage.

▶ Window boxes present the opportunity for seasonal change. I kept the windows simple: double-hung on the first floor.

Annuals bloom all summer long. Purple cabbage, mums, and vines usher in autumn and dwarf evergreens in winter might even be delicately lighted. However, window boxes demand watering and upkeep; the contents mustn't be allowed to get spindly or brown. Look at your boxes from afar to make sure that they are well mounted and aren't tilted or drooping. Anything added to the façade of the home should bring a dash of panache.

Knock on Wood

Make sure your guests and family aren't knocking on vinyl when they come to call. Of course there is nothing like the solid-wood, raised-panel door original to a house, but good reproductions are available. I treat exterior doors in one of three ways, going from the simplest to the most lavish: stripped and unfinished, left raw and primitive; stained and varnished in a flat finish; or painted brightly using semigloss in red, black, white, or yellow. Coordinate the door to the style of the house, just as you would shoes to an outfit: rustic little cottage with raw pine; colonial farmhouse wearing a darkly stained panel; Georgian-style manse dressed in elegant red.

Farmhouses of yore often had kitchen doors, or mudrooms, yet were dark because they lacked windows. Replacing a solid door with a glass-paneled door in the kitchen will let in all available light. (An ornamental gate added a layer of security in the Washington, D.C., townhouse.) Dutch doors—doors cut in half widthwise—offer light and the ability to keep an eye on small children or pets outside.

I feel a tug of nostalgia at the sound of a slammed screen door. Summer days, a ticking sprinkler, crackly voiced play-by-plays from a transistor radio, watermelon seeds, and wet suits flung on the clothes line—they're all ushered back in a single slam. Screen doors must be wood, and in my book, it's okay if they've been repaired, even crudely. Remember the odd patch somebody sewed over a hole? You can still find good wooden screen doors from the 1930s and '40s at flea markets and garage sales. Cover the bottom half with an extra layer of small-squared chicken wire, and they'll be invincible to children and pets.

Roofing

When presented with the dubious task of replacing a roof, I usually choose one of the following three: cedar, slate, or asphalt shingle. How do I decide? Cedar is more expensive than asphalt, so when cost is a factor I'll opt for asphalt. (And yet the muse of economy ponders: cedar, while costing more initially, lasts longer. She would probably opt for cedar for a long-term solution.) Cedar or asphalt work well on farmhouses, cottages, colonials—houses all simple to moderate in style. (With asphalt, the less complicated the design, the better. Fancier, cut-out styles look more like reproductions.) I save slate, which is cleaner and dressier, for more important architecture, such as the stylized design of Georgian or Greek Revival. Cedar, slate, and asphalt shingles all come in a selection of colors. Stick with black, tan, or gray colored shingles unless the façade is white, in which case consider red or green. One final option for humbler abodes is tin. Imagine the sound of the rain on your summer cabin or cottage.

▶ The Iowa farmhouse roof was covered in asphalt shingle for a sense of simplicity.

Your Own Backyard

Grass is underrated. Our excessive times seem to demand goldfish ponds and multitiered decks, stone gazebos and lush landscaping. Woe to the Jones who is happy with a simple expanse of beautiful green grass; what an underachiever he would seem. My ideal is the proverbial white picket fence, a low-slung stone wall, or the wooded glen that existed before the house was built and will, with any luck, exist there long after. I don't lay claims to having any landscaping talents and am certainly in favor of greenery, but the balanced, building-hugging shrubbery of the suburban tract home is not for me. Give me an English country garden, which appears—in all its haphazard jocularity—to have been sewn by a madwoman in a windstorm, all thistle and Queen Anne's Lace and crooked tea-rose bush vying for the sun. (I know, I know; the amount of planning that went into the appearance of such confusion was extraordinary.) The point is nothing in the yard should look too cute, too planned, too balanced. And the consumer warning on lawn ornaments should read something like this: "Use *extreme* caution when handling, buying, or placing in yard. May cause undue tackiness, silliness, or cutesiness." The same disdain should be directed toward plastic garden containers, outsized fencing, large inappropriate

▲ I leave many properties the way I found them as far as the grounds go: a lawn of simple grass and shade trees can't be beat.

sculptures (lions as sentry to a humble ranch), or anything, really, that calls too much attention to itself.

My favorite driveway (who but me has a favorite driveway?) consists of two worn treadmarks, one on either side of a median, the grass of which is kept low from brushing against the car's chassis. The treads might contain gravel or they might be worn smooth, but there's always grass in between. With any luck, the driveway is long and winding. For me, the sound of gravel crunching beneath the wheels of the family vehicle is the equivalent of Proust's madeleines in evoking childhood memories. There were chilly nights, asleep in the backseat of the station wagon, when the abrupt end of tires on gravel, the slight skid of tire against stone meant that we were home again. Or the sound of an approaching vehicle crunching up the driveway sounded a portent of grocery bags or guests. Perhaps memories must be sacrificed since gravel isn't always practical. (It can shift, creating bald spots, and can be problematic on hilly terrain.) Use asphalt if you must and give it a gravel coat. A driveway of black asphalt or cement is anathema to me. It harkens supermarkets, freeways, and industrial complexes.

▶ Whether picket, at right, or plank, above right, these driveway gates charm.

At the end of the driveway stood a garage, low-slung but with a peaked, shingled roof and a set of bifold doors that swung open to reveal my grandfather's curvaceous and gleaming Oldsmobile. There was always a flattened cardboard box on the floor to catch the car's oil drippings and a ladder that pulled down from the ceiling, allowing me to climb up into the cramped eaves of the attic. I loved that garage, the chill of it, the metallic smell of it, the chance it afforded me to dwell in secret for a while.

Give in to the convenience of an electronic garage door but cover it with reproduction foldaways to retain the charm of a period garage. I love garages with peaked roofs, rows of second-story windows, and the potential to house a studio or mini-apartment. If you have a separate garage built in the same period as the house, paint it in the same hue as the main building and cover it with the same roof material.

▼ This wonderful three-car garage is part of a barn.

In Conclusion

Remember: The simpler the house, the less complicated the embellishments should be, including the color, material, and fixtures. You shouldn't try to force a plain cottage on a small plot of land into something it is not. Whenever I choose a color or a texture to add to a house exterior I stop and think: would this have been viable seventy years ago? Would my machinations put a frown on the original owner's face or would he approve? Is it because I love old houses so dearly that I can't ignore the presence of owners past who seem to hover at my side? Whatever it is, I am indebted to the past and to a sense that the historical importance of a structure should be honored and held, to some degree, in awe. Perhaps that is why I am fascinated with period photographs of houses and seek them out whenever possible. I am particularly pleased when there are period images of the houses I have purchased. There, frozen before me, is the way the house was intended to look and be used. While not entirely wedded to a precise reconstruction, I am definitely informed by the images and ideas that I see there. Usually, successive renovations—purported to have added to the home—have in fact detracted, made the impact *less* by adding more. My mission, then, is to restore the simplicity of the house, to pay homage to a time without excess.

▲ A trim little garage; the latticework in the foreground is wood, of course.

▶ Outbuildings must have character. This corncrib in Iowa has loads.

Let's Go Shopping—
Hunting and
Gathering

10

*Only a fool thinks price and value
are the same.*
—Antonio Machado

◀ From flea markets to antique shops,
rummage sales to thrift stores, I am an
inveterate shopper. There's a wealth of
shops and markets in Iowa.

Many readers will know by now

that most of the objects and furnishings pictured here are preowned collectibles, antiques, or found items. A lifetime of collecting has uncovered most of the treasures with which I decorate.

The first question a visitor asks upon entering one of my homes is typically "Where did you get all this stuff?" Driven as I am by the three muses of comfort, color, and economy, I'm always on the lookout for decorative additions that bring an interesting look without breaking the bank. Friends and family have learned that it is nearly impossible for me to drive by a garage sale without stopping. Flea markets are hunted down like exotic game and pounced on in the wee hours of the morning when some of the best items and best deals can

be had. Thrift stores and junk and antiques shops are mined for possible gems. And I don't entirely reject the new: I regularly haunt sales tables and clearance rooms at major furniture retailers. Although some of my loved ones will cringe when I admit it, I've also been known to rescue items from the neighbor's trash. Why should a perfectly good chair or table be shunned simply because of its humble provenance?

▶ Repeated visits to flea markets rewarded me with this white ironstone pitcher and, most certainly, stacks of dishes.

How to See

Shopping can be overwhelming. Whether you're shopping for towels or a side table for your living room, so many possibilities exist. How to cut through the clutter? "Beginners" accompanying me for a Saturday of hunting are overwhelmed by the tables heaped with household goods, glassware, books, jewelry, and knickknacks. I'll pick up a piece of art pottery culled from what appears to be useless dreck, and he or she will ask, "How did you see it?" The art of successful flea marketing is really the art of seeing. I believe it is a skill as easy to cultivate as it is to be born with. Learning to see is simply a matter of willingness and practice, and it is a crucial skill when shopping at a flea market or thrift store, where so much of the stuff is literally junk or else not on your agenda.

How to discern the objects of your desire? Make a list of the things you want or need; the mere act of compiling it will help narrow your focus. If chairs are on your list, scan immediately for groups of furniture at an outdoor market. Make your way around the entire market looking only at chairs. Your energy is thus devoted to one objective, allowing you to ignore tabletops of glassware or old iron bedsteads. I have developed the ability to simultaneously hunt for many of the objects I collect, including objects I don't yet collect, as my collections are always expanding. If I can develop the ability to see, so can you. It is simply a matter of having some idea of what it is you're looking for, and then, once finding it, using a few other criteria.

Where to Shop

- Flea markets. Don't be afraid to dicker.

- Garage and house sales. Get there early!

- Thrift stores, such as Goodwill and Salvation Army.

- Antiques and collectibles stores. Check out the antiques malls that house multiple dealers.

- Auctions. Examine the items beforehand and keep a level head during the bidding.

- Online auctions. Ask lots of questions before bidding.

- Sales tables and clearance rooms of furniture retailers.

- Church bazaars and street fairs.

- Moving sales in apartment buildings.

- The sidewalks on trash day. Remember, you're recycling!

Is This the Right Chair?

Three things I keep in mind when deciding to purchase an object are its design, its age, and the material with which it is made. Cost, of course, always plays a role and is one of the reasons I buy used objects and collectibles.

The Shape of Things—Design

The manner in which something is designed is the first thing that draws me to it. I look for interesting shapes, be it in a vase, a lamp base, or in the legs of a chair. A certain voluptuousness might draw me to a vase, or the bulbous feet of a little wooden stool might have a visual pull. Simple lines from nature, grids from geometry, the arcs and gullies of the human form might take my eye. Look for shapes that attract you, lines that are simple, design that stands alone. Think about height and width in terms of the way certain objects fill the air. You may need tall, thin objects in certain spaces to pull the eye up. Alternatively, a wider, chubbier piece might fill the void beneath a table or fit an open space on a bookshelf. Good design is not only about

▶ Collect interesting, oddly shaped chairs to vary the visual impact.

editing but also about putting the pieces of a puzzle together.

Good design is enhanced through workmanship. Look for strength in furniture, smoothness in pottery, a tight weave in fabrics and textiles, and again, an overall simplicity in the way in which the object was put together.

Handmade can be better, although great objects emerged from the 1950s and the streamlined assembly lines of the decades following. Good workmanship usually has a certain heft, a lack of flimsiness, and a quality of feeling good in the hand.

Color is a design choice. When you look at

◀ Don't be overwhelmed by all the clutter. You will learn how to discern the gems from the junk.

▼ Keep detailed notes when you visit the flea market. That way you can come back later for items you really want and can afford.

▼ The perfect design . . . for a grand bunch of flowers or bundle of kindling. This container was probably used in a former life to empty the contents of chamber pots.

an object's design, consider the color. Do you like it? Does it fit within the family of hues in the room in which you plan to use it? Look for true, natural color. Of course, you can always paint an object if the color is garish or wrong. But remember, if the object is from a certain period and the paint is original, it may be wise to leave it as is.

Signatures, hallmarks, and dates on objects often (but not always) herald good design. Look on the bottom of a chair for a maker or label; turn over a vase or piece of pottery for a mark or imprint that may be the sign of a famous designer. The mark shouldn't determine whether or not you like a piece but may convince you to buy a piece you're on the fence about purchasing. Signed pieces are typically worth more than those that are not. Educate yourself about hallmarks, logos, and signatures, and your shopping excursions will be more lucrative and fun.

▼ Design and practicality are married in this bulbous chrome coffeemaker from the 1950s. Blue-and-white china patterns were ubiquitous in the '40s and '50s.

▶ The dings and mottling on pieces of white enamelware only add to their beauty. And don't be afraid to leave paintings unframed. In this setting, a frame would appear pretentious.

How Old is It?

Age is one of the criteria I use when buying decorative objects. Since I so rarely purchase new things, the age of an object is inherently a consideration. I like antiques, which in the United States have to be at least 100 years old to be considered such. I also enjoy collectibles, objects, and furniture from the 1930s through the '60s. You can often tell an object's age simply by the type of object that it is. A pink Princess dial telephone is obviously from the early '60s, whereas a Bakelite radio dates from the '40s. Other clues to age might be as obvious as a copyright date or a patent number engraved on the object. Excessive wear or darkened rings on pottery indicate age. Woodcarvings tend to darken and crack as they get older. Certain materials such as ebony, ivory, Bakelite, and early plastic are rarely used today, having been replaced by technological advances or rendered unseemly because of endangered species or diminishing rain forests. Another clue to age is the manner of construction. Machines changed the way furniture was made, as did the factory assembly line. Furniture that is rough hewn, has dovetailed joints, lacks screws, and is thoroughly worn on the seat or the handrails *may* be handmade. Keep in mind that antiques are expensive, difficult to find, and vastly reproduced. What may look to the untrained eye as "old" may simply be a good reproduction. In order to thwart disappointment, buy what you love, can afford, and will use. You won't go wrong.

◀ The 1950s jockey is a favorite flea-market find.

What's It Made Of?

I look for materials of substance. I choose solid wood over ply, stainless steel over plastic, ceramic tile over linoleum. That's not to say that mid-century materials aren't to be valued or used.

▼ At an Iowa flea market I examined a dresser to see how it was made before making an offer.

A Lucite lamp base, Bakelite pulls for a dresser, or colored glass from the 1960s make stunning additions to a rural retreat.

▼ Discuss delivery charges before you purchase a large piece. Delivery can be more expensive than the piece itself. Use delivery cost as part of your overall negotiation: You might meet the dealer's price for the item but insist that delivery be included.

Buy What You Love.

Remember that in the end, you are buying objects and furniture to live with. You want your family to feel cared for, your friends to be comforted, your home to be warm and accessible. All the design and buying tips in the world won't assemble a wonderful home if you haven't purchased things you love. Love what you buy. Feel an insatiable pull toward a table lamp or chair before you lay your money down.

Think about where the object is going to fit in your home, and if you can come up with three spots where it will be just fabulous, then make an offer. The only buying mistakes I ever made were those in which I wasn't in love with the object at hand. You know love when you feel it.

A running theme in these pages is that the three simple ideals of color, economy, and

▼ A cherished find: my 1940s sofa. I left it as is.

▼ A designer's dress form serves as an impromptu sculpture and picks up the theme of the human form in the photograph above.

The Art of Seeing

- Use these criteria to help decide whether an object is worth your attention and money:

- Design: Is it timeless and well proportioned?

- Shape: Are you drawn to the shape of it? Does it fill the air well?

- Workmanship: Is it strong and simply made?

- Color: Do you like the color? Will it work with your room's tones?

- Signatures or hallmarks: Are there identifying marks or signatures?

- Age: Older things tend to be better made. If you're a collector you'll want the item to be of the period in which you collect.

- Material: What's it made of? You probably wouldn't want brass in a bathroom full of chrome. Solid wood is better than plywood. Does the material have heft and quality?

- Love: Am I drawn to this object? Is it love?

▶ Portraits of characters unknown are fun to collect. I try to invent biographies for each one. These portraits were picked out of the trash in New York City.

◀ ▼ Look for objects that pull their weight: well designed and functional. The lidless coffeepot (left) and the vintage lard container (below) were useful then and are useful now.

Flea Market Strategies

Before you go . . .

- Make a list of items you want or need.

- Take along measurements for tables, rugs, window treatments, rooms, and ceiling heights.

- Think about colors and hues you want.

- Be prepared to transport larger purchases . . . or pay more to have them delivered.

- Take along plenty of cash, which dealers prefer over credit cards or checks.

- Get there early to get the best buys.

- Wear comfortable shoes and a hat to ward off the sun.

While you shop . . .

- Don't be afraid to dicker over the price.

- Inspect an item carefully before buying. (Be aware of chips, flaws, loose joints; merchandise is sold "as is" and is generally not returnable.)

- If you like it, buy it, as it won't be there for long.

- Look into boxes and beneath tables for objects difficult to display.

- Move quickly.

comfort—personified as muses—inform every design and restoration decision I make. And so it is that my interpretation of these ideals seems to manifest itself in a rural sensibility. The muse economy has risen prominently here. While I agree with Webster's Seventh New Collegiate Dictionary that she represents " . . . the thrifty use of material resources," to me she represents much more. I've written much about hunting and gathering, shopping and buying, and yet most of these objects have been here long before us and will be here long after. We're not talking about ownership as much as guardianship. Recycling and reuse were important tenets of farmers and of people who worked the land. Again the frugality and practicality of my grandmother come to mind. To cherish and pass along these objects of age and quality is to pay homage to both the object and to the people who used them. So economy, much like country, is a state of mind.

▶ Another delectable flea-market find that I bought and would have chosen to reupholster, but never did. I keep it on display in my Iowa living room.

11

A Country State of Mind

Teach us to delight in simple things.
—Rudyard Kipling,
"The Children's Song,"
Puck of Pook's Hill

◀ The simplicity in color and design
of this barn is a thing divine.

Although there is no substitute for a rustic

barn and the sight of cattle grazing on the hillside, a cold-water brook stocked with trout, or a general store whose shelves abound with local jams and honey, "country" might best be acknowledged as a state of mind. My grandmother lived on a farm nearly her whole life; it wasn't until later that she left the farm for a place in town. But she is famous for her treks back to the country for a freshly slaughtered chicken; she still cans and puts in supplies for the winter, still crochets blankets for each new addition to growing generations. She's long since left the country, and yet the values instilled by rural living remain with her, true and strong.

In these pages I've tried to show you how to bring country simplicity into your life by using color, comfort, and economy. But I would like to think that larger ideas loom between these concepts. For instance, I always opt for thrift over excess, quality over quantity, thoughtfulness instead of impulse, and elbow grease and reuse rather than purchasing the new. I also feel indebted to those who came before us, not simply for the structures and artifacts they left behind but also for the single-mindedness with which they pursued a simple life. Surely these are values that we can all regard highly as Americans, whether we're from the city or the country or from a place in between. If the so-called country lifestyle has one message that can be universally applied no matter where one hangs one's hat it might be to live simply. Use what you need. Reject pomp. Which is not to imply that one should go without but instead develop a keen and deft hand at paring away. So the muse of economy is one of value, not miserliness. It's knowing when to spend a little

▶ Although temporary, this stack of linens makes an interesting textural sculpture in its own right.

more, and when to hold back. Remember: you will need to develop your own sense of decorating values as you proceed. Let the muses guide you.

Another tenet of rural life that can inform your decorating style is hospitality: the belief that neighborliness and an extended hand are an integral part of living on the land. When I speak of comfort as one of the three design muses, I'm not merely thinking about plump sofa cushions and freshly laundered linen. Welcoming people into your home is saying, in effect, that you wish to offer comfort. You will proffer that downy pillow for a back; freshly brewed tea will appear in china cups (however mismatched!);

something homemade will be presented and enjoyed. And yet it is you they've come to see, your children and pets they want to know about, your friendship they seek. When we take the time to think about how our home looks, how it smells, how it feels to the limbs of the weary, we express quite directly that we value others. When we open our homes to share our family rituals and celebrations we show how intensely we care. We care for the opinions, comforts, and concerns of those outside our circle. We want to know and experience the lives of others, and we want them to know and experience our lives as well. Hospitality laced with generosity is very much a part of a "country" state of mind.

The Muses Speak

Color

I am the brazen punch of bright pastels and I am also the soft, muted glow of a table lamp in a window, as seen from the road. The clarity and unfussiness of white in all its guises is me. Variegated hues of wood worn—by footfalls or fingers?—down to the grain become me. I am just the trace of color, color faded through service and utility, transparent color, color drawn from the palette of nature. I am color, compatible and uncomplicated.

Economy

I am all things worn but strong, old but working. I am all good material that lasts. Call me patience. Call me restraint. I know the difference between generosity and waste. I reject both excess and miserliness.

Comfort

I am softness sublime, unfussy and accessible. Cotton and linen and silk define me. Children of all ages befriend me. I never intimidate, only welcome. I am the hand extended in friendship, the food offered to restore. I am the hearth fire or the humble stove. I am the opening of a door, the vulnerability of the heart.

A Rural Connection—How to Bring the Country into Your Home

- Have fun. Decorating should be joyful and energizing. If you find yourself dreading every decision, you're taking it way too seriously.

- Buy what you love. Don't choose "make-do" pieces that you're not in love with unless they fulfill some practical purpose.

- Be patient. A room is an organic thing. It doesn't have to reach a point of perfection at which you stop. Let your space evolve with your changing lifestyle, family, and budget.

- Replace pieces when you're able to and when you fall in love with something new. (I often sell pieces I've fallen out of love with and use the proceeds to upgrade to the new.)

- Buy original art if possible. I'd rather buy a verging-on-tacky oil painting of flowers at a flea market than a poster of a Monet from the museum. Group all those 1950s flower paintings together on the wall and you'll have a charming gallery.

- Make yourself comfortable. It's your home after all; make sure your seating and beds are comforting retreats.

- Steal ideas from books (such as this one) and magazines, but make sure your own personality shows through.

- Have some sense of the period of your house or rooms. You needn't be wedded to its restoration or hamstrung by the period's design; just have some sense of it and lean toward it when in doubt.

- Mix the new with the old, including periods, styles, colors and patterns.

- Relinquish the notion of keeping up with anyone or anything but your own heart.

- Remember the three muses of comfort, economy, and color and conjure them up for decorating sessions or shopping sprees. Or better yet, develop muses of your own and call on them for inspiration and your own sense of style.

▶ This space, for me, reveals the essentials of a welcoming country home, with its focus on comfort and its rustic furniture that mix well with the clean, canvas-white background. Don't rush outdoors just yet. Take a moment to rest on the upholstered bench and reflect on the crisp fall day.

Appendix

Before You Begin: Some Concerns

All the body-wearying toil that it took to restore my farmhouse in Iowa taught me that making things simpler, in effect taking things away, is a lot of work. Whether removing siding to reveal Nineteenth-century clapboard, or ripping up '50s linoleum to expose genuine tile, restorative labor is never easy. It can also be dangerous. Before you start on any project you've never done before, no matter how simple it may appear, consult an expert. Ask questions. Find out from someone who has done the same sort of job about what it entails.

When I wanted poured concrete counters in the kitchen of my townhouse in Harlem, I didn't ponder for a second whether to tackle the job myself. Recognize when a task is too big or too complex for you and call in the experts. It is one thing to paper a wall and quite another to erect one.

Practice your skills on smaller projects before taking on the big one. If you've never refinished a piece of furniture, don't start with your beloved grandmother's rocking chair. Start with something simple and familiarize yourself with wood grains and with sanding, stripping, and refinishing products. Practice working with stains and paint

colors on small unobtrusive patches of the piece before covering it completely. Make sure you're pleased with the product when it has dried.

Recognize the importance of every step of a project. In order for paint to adhere, wood furniture must nearly always be sanded, which is laborious and in some cases difficult. Do you have the patience to do the job the right way? If not, and no sin in this, perhaps you should hire a professional to do it.

Wear protective clothing, shoes, and gloves, and use safety goggles when handling tools. Get the right tools for the task and learn how to use them efficiently. If you are uncertain how a particular tool works, ask someone who knows to teach you. Proper tools can make the difference between a mediocre job and a good one, but you must know how to use them. The right tool, used correctly, also increases the level of safety.

Familiarize yourself with the products you use and be sure to read the manufacturers' directions, warnings, and cautions. Certain products must be used out of doors and adhere best in low humidity. Read all labels and heed all warnings.

Be particularly vigilant of noxious fumes and the need for circulating air. Paint stripper can be toxic. And it's not just the fumes that are dangerous. Chemicals and toxins from the fluid can leach directly into the skin through work gloves. Make sure you are protected or look for the less toxic brands that are touted as noncarcenogenic.

Cautions at a Glance

- Never expose babies or small children to lead-based paint.

- Educate yourself about asbestos and consult a professional with regard to its removal.

- Read the labels and heed the warnings on all paint and refinishing products.

- If you don't know how a particular tool works, don't use it.

- Protect yourself with the appropriate safety wear, goggles, and gloves.

- Never plug in the frayed or damaged cords of older electrical appliances.

- Take care when installing electrical appliances around areas where water will be used.

- Get an expert to check out a vintage stove before using it.

- Don't use vintage ceramic plate ware to heat or serve food. The glazes may contain toxins.

- Hire a professional for the big jobs.

- Check local building codes and ordinances before beginning a project.

Educate yourself about asbestos, a mineral fiber often used as insulation in homes built between 1930 and 1950. Ingesting asbestos fiber increases the risk of lung cancer. Products that may have contained asbestos include, but are not limited to, pipes, boilers, ducts, floor tiles, cement sheets, millboard, soundproofing, patching and joint compounds, and roofing, shingles, and siding. Don't try to remove suspected asbestos materials as tears or cuts are prone to release the asbestos fibers. Removal of asbestos-laden materials must be performed by a professional. (Contact the U.S. Consumer Product Safety Commission at 1-800-638-CPSC for more information.)

Never use fixtures, furniture, or objects with lead paint, peeling paint, or rust around babies, toddlers, or young children. Lead-based paint and lead-based paint dust are extremely dangerous when inhaled or ingested. Babies and young children are particularly vulnerable to the toxins found in lead-based paint. Although I discuss many examples of furniture on which the original paint is peeling, I cannot under-score enough how important it is to protect children from the hazard of lead-based paint. Lead-based paint was used in many homes built prior to 1978, the year the federal government banned it. Any restoration work in older homes must take into account the possibility of lead-based paint. (Contact the National Lead Information Center for more information on how to protect your family: 1-800-LEAD-FYI.)

I frequently use lamps, fans, and other electrical devices from the '30s and '40s but am extremely conscientious when it comes to safety. Never plug in an electrical cord that is damaged or frayed. Lamps are easy to rewire, and if you don't have the confidence to do it yourself, the service is rather inexpensive. Older fans can be dangerous to use if you have children or pets about. The grill on older models doesn't prevent small fingers or tails from poking through. Be on the safe side and don't use them around small creatures.

Index

Acknowledgements

Without Nancy Becker, this book would exist only in my mind. Kudos and heartfelt thanks to her for putting it on the page. Love and appreciation to Nancy Soriano and all the folks at *Country Living* magazine who have encouraged and supported me throughout the years. The helpful and sound words of advice from Jacqueline Deval at Hearst Books were a calming and guiding presence throughout the book-writing process. And thanks to all the editors, stylists, and photographers whose special skills and talents put me in the best possible light. Last but not least, thanks to all the builders who turned my vision into reality.

Photography Credits

The Publisher would like to thank the following photographers for supplying the pictures in this book:

Page 1 Bill Milne; **2** Ryan Benyi; **5** Ryan Benyi; **6,7 top** Keith Scott Morton; **7 bottom** Steve Gross & Sue Daley; **8** Keith Scott Morton; **10, 12, 13, 14** Steve Gross & Sue Daley; **16, 18, 19 left** Kevin Schwasinger; **19 right** Steve Gross & Sue Daley; **20** Kevin Schwasinger; **21, 22** Keith Scott Morton; **23** Michael Weschler; **24** Keith Scott Morton; **26** Keith Scott Morton; **27, 28** Steve Gross & Sue Daley; **30, 32** Kevin Schwasinger; **33, 34, 35** Steve Gross & Sue Daley; **36, 37** Keith Scott Morton; **38 left** Kevin Schwasinger; **38 right, 39** Keith Scott Morton; **40, left** Steve Gross & Sue Daley; **40 right** Keith Scott Morton; **41, 42** Kevin Schwasinger; **43, 44** Steve Gross & Sue Daley; **46, 47** Kevin Schwasinger; **48** Steve Gross & Sue Daley; **49 left** Kevin Schwasinger; **49 right** Keith Scott Morton; **50** Steve Gross & Sue Daley; **51** Michael Weschler; **54** Steve Gross & Sue Daley; **56** Keith Scott Morton; **57** Kevin Schwasinger; **58, 59, 61, 62, 64** Steve Gross & Sue Daley; **65, 67** Michael Weschler; **68** Kevin Schwasinger; **70** Keith Scott Morton; **71 top** Kevin Schwasinger; **71 middle** Keith Scott Morton; **71 bottom** Kevin Schwasinger; **72, 73** Keith Scott Morton; **74** Kevin Schwasinger; **75 left** Keith Scott Morton; **75 right, 76, 77** Steve Gross & Sue Daley; **78** Michael Weschler; **81** Keith Scott Morton; **82, 83 top** Michael Weschler; **83 left** Steve Gross & Sue Daley; **83 right** Kevin Schwasinger; **84** Steve Gross & Sue Daley; **85 left** Kevin Schwasinger; **85 right, 86** Steve Gross & Sue Daley; **87** Michael Weschler; **88 top** Kevin Schwasinger; **88 bottom** Keith Scott Morton; **89 top right** Kevin Schwasinger; **89 bottom left** Keith Scott Morton; **90, 92 top, 92 bottom** Steve Gross & Sue Daley; **93** Michael Weschler; **94** Steve Gross & Sue Daley; **97** Keith Scott Morton; **98, 101, 103** Kevin Schwasinger; **105** Michael Weschler; **107, 109** Keith Scott Morton; **111 left** Steve Gross & Sue Daley; **111 right** Keith Scott Morton; **112, 115** Steve Gross & Sue Daley; **117** Keith Scott Morton; **119** Kevin Schwasinger; **120** Steve Gross & Sue Daley; **121** Michael Weschler; **122, 123** Kevin Schwasinger; **124** Steve Gross & Sue Daley; **125, 126, 127, 128** Kevin Schwasinger; **129** Michael Weschler; **130, 132, 133, 135 left** Keith Scott Morton; **135 right, 136, 137** Kevin Schwasinger; **139, 140, 141 left** Keith Scott Morton; **141 right, 142** Keith Scott Morton; **143** Keith Scott Morton; **144** Steve Gross & Sue Daley; **147, 149** Kevin Schwasinger; **151** Michael Weschler; **152, 154, 155, 156, 157, 158** Kevin Schwasinger; **159** Steve Gross & Sue Daley; **160** Michael Weschler; **163, 165** Kevin Schwasinger; **166, 167 left** Michael Weschler; **167 right, 168** Kevin Schwasinger; **169** Keith Scott Morton; **170** Steve Gross & Sue Daley; **171** Michael Weschler; **172, 173, 174, 175, 177, 178** Kevin Schwasinger; **181** Keith Scott Morton; **182, 183 top** Steve Gross & Sue Daley; **183 bottom** Kevin Schwasinger; **185, 186** Keith Scott Morton